BOY IN THE CUPBOARD

BOY IN THE CUPBOARD

SHANE DUNPHY ～

Gill & Macmillan

Gill & Macmillan Ltd
Hume Avenue, Park West, Dublin 12
with associated companies throughout the world
www.gillmacmillan.ie

978 07171 4651 2
First published 2009
First published in this format 2010

Typography design by Make Communication
Print origination by O'K Graphic Design, Dublin
Printed in the UK by CPI Cox and Wyman, Reading

The paper used in this book comes from the wood pulp
of managed forests. For every tree felled, at least one
tree is planted, thereby renewing natural resources.

A CIP catalogue record for this book is available from
the British Library.

5 4 3 2 1

For Deirdre—you make me feel lucky

I said: 'My bonny Creole girl, my money here's no good.
If it weren't for the alligators, I'd sleep out in the wood.'

'You're welcome here, kind stranger—our house is very plain;
But me mammy welcomes strangers in, on the banks of
Ponchartrain.'

'The Lakes of Ponchartrain', TRADITIONAL FOLK SONG FROM
THE SINGING OF CHRISTY MOORE

PROLOGUE

Melanie Moorehouse had the Indigo Girls playing quietly over the stereo system in her Hyundai coupé. They were singing about being in love with a ghost, close harmonies soaring over intricate acoustic guitars, but I was barely listening. I slumped low in the passenger seat, my nerves jangling and my stomach rolling with hunger and acid, my muscles tight with anxiety. I had slept little over the past three days, and every moment of wakefulness was taking its toll on me as we sped along in the early evening. I gazed through the narrow car windows: houses and office blocks had long given way to fields and hedgerows. We were climbing now, going up into the mountains, the city falling away behind us in the distance.

'Can't you make this bucket go any faster?' I growled, fighting the panic that was welling up inside me, threatening to overflow.

'I can, but not without killing us both, Shane,' Melanie said, glancing at me from the corner of her eye. 'Just sit tight. We'll be there in ten minutes.'

The road, little more than a pathway with grass growing in the middle, curled, serpentine, into a series of dangerous bends. I closed my eyes and tried to focus on breathing. If luck smiled on us, we would not be too late.

Maybe I slept for a time, exhaustion sneaking up on me; perhaps I turned awareness inside in an attempt to hide from reality—either way, we had suddenly arrived. A large Victorian edifice rose out of wild overgrown countryside, with arched Gothic windows like alien eyes peering down on the bright pink sports car. I pushed open the car door and stepped out stiffly. Melanie dialled the office on her mobile phone. I heard her speaking as I painfully climbed the rickety fence because the gate was rusted shut and began to limp up the dirt path to the front door, an ornate thing of darkened oak, hanging on its hinges.

'Mrs Munro, could you please tell Ben we've arrived ... No ... It looks like we've missed them ... Sure, sure, I'll call you as soon as we're certain.' A pause. 'No, he's okay. Look, I'd better go.'

She followed me, running to catch up. I stood in the doorway, feeling nausea gather in the pit of my abdomen. Inside the derelict house I could hear water dripping, the creaking of old wood, and behind that a thick, pervasive silence.

'What do you think?' Melanie asked, at my shoulder now.

'I think we'd better check for certain,' I said, and stepped over the threshold into the dusty interior.

It was dark and musty inside; the smell of damp and filth hung heavily in the air. The hallway seemed to be impossibly wide and deep, as if the inner shell of the house had been constructed along a kind of open plan, unheard of at the time this monolith had been built. My boots crackled over grit and broken tiles. A room opened up to my right, a crumbling fireplace set into a wall that had wisps of wallpaper peeling from it. The roof was high above, and suddenly I realised what was missing. A landing jutted above me, but no stairs led up to it.

'The stairway is gone,' I said to Melanie, motioning with my head.

'So is a lot of the woodwork—look.'

She was right. I noticed that door frames, skirting boards and even some of the flooring had been pulled up—and recently. Splinters and bits of nail protruded, obviously fresh.

'Why would they do that?' Melanie asked me.

'I've seen Travellers who aren't accustomed to living in houses use the wood from stairs and windowsills to light the fire,' I said, continuing to move along the hall, checking the rooms to my right and left. 'They seem to equate it with using scrub from the ditches where they're camping to fuel the stove in the evenings. But Collette and Marius aren't Travellers. It doesn't make much sense.'

There was a door at the end of the hall, and I pushed it open with my foot. Immediately a foul stench assailed us—it was difficult to say what it was exactly. It was as though something had been lying dead for a long time and had started to dry up. But there was also the raw odour of ammonia, and the underlying reek of human waste. Trying hard not to gag, I put the sleeve of my leather jacket over my nose and mouth and went inside. Melanie was behind me.

The room had once been a kitchen. There were the remains of a sink, an old Aga and some cupboards and storage units now mostly dismantled. A space to the left contained a rickety wooden table, and a couple of chairs had been overturned near it. The smell was emanating from a crater that had been dug in the floor, which had been stripped of all boards and coverings down to the bare earth. A substance that looked not unlike oil seemed to have been deposited into this hole, which took up most of the vast kitchen.

'Shane, why is it moving?' Melanie asked me, her voice shaking.

'What do you mean?' I said impatiently, and then I saw she was right.

The black puddle was swaying and rolling before my eyes as if it was a single, living organism. For a moment I had a sickening sense of vertigo, my mind desperately trying to process what I was seeing. Then I became aware of something else, a noise in the background, a gentle, droning *buzz* that was rising in pitch and becoming more ferocious. Suddenly, I knew what we were looking at.

'I think we should leave,' I said, starting to push Melanie backwards gently.

'Why—' she said, but then realisation dawned on her, too. 'Oh my *God* ...'

This final ejaculation was our undoing. The black mass, thousands of flies that had settled on the shit and piss in the trough, which had been dug in the kitchen floor for use as a toilet, rose into the air in a cloud—a swirling, frenetic vortex. Melanie started to scream uncontrollably, clinging to me and beating against me with her fists at the same time. I tried to grasp her shoulders to steer her out of the doorway, but she had frozen in panic and wouldn't move. Just as the first wave of insects descended, a baby started to cry somewhere above us.

Chapter 1 ~

TWO MONTHS EARLIER

The Tomescu family were Romanian, and had arrived in the city on a ferry from Liverpool a year before. Elvira and Petru, the parents, were in their mid-twenties and had the peaked, jaundiced look of people who had seen far too much hardship in their young lives. Their son, whom they insisted on referring to as Craig, although he spoke no English, was three. The Tomescus moved from one grotty bedsit to the next in their first six months in Ireland as Petru lurched through a series of ill-paid jobs. He quickly developed a reputation: he was dour, seemed to carry a sense of barely repressed violence about with him and it was rumoured he had allied himself with some of the numerous Eastern European criminal gangs. He was linked to several criminal acts, one involving the brutal beating and rape of a sixteen-year-old boy during a botched robbery. If he was involved in any illegal enterprises, however, he had been very careful, and the police had been unable to convict him of anything. It was during this time that I first encountered the family.

Craig was attending a pre-school crèche while his mother worked as a chambermaid at a local hotel. His behaviour was causing the staff some concerns. At my boss's request, I visited one morning, and was met by Irma, the manager. She was a large, red-faced woman in her late thirties, and she exuded a sense of motherliness.

'Craig is still very much removed from the other children,' she told me as we sat in her small office, 'but there's more to it than that. He's exhibiting some classic signs of neglect.'

'Such as?'

She stood up and opened the door. 'Come and see for yourself.'

The main play area was brightly decorated, and divided into several sections, each designated for specific activities: dress-up, home corner, messy play, story time, music and quiet time. That morning, there were fourteen children and three staff dotted about the room, all engaged in various play exercises, and there was a pleasant buzz of conversation. This was a busy, happy, well-run establishment. As I cast my eyes about the room, I could see everything was clean, there was plenty of light and space, radiators, sockets and any sharp corners were covered and made safe—and most importantly, the children all seemed happy and relaxed. All but one.

I stood at the door with Irma, and was immediately able to pick Craig out. While every other child was in a group, hard at play, he was off to the side, observing everything that was going on around the room, but very much alone.

'That him?' I asked, motioning with my head.

'Yes,' Irma said. 'Now, watch carefully.'

It was hard to tell if Craig was small for his age or not. He was sitting against the wall in the home corner, his arms wrapped about his knees, his eyes wide and hollow. His hair, which was a tawny brown colour, had been cropped close to his skull, and his clothes were scuffed and ill-fitting. His eyes were glued to the activities of the other children, yet he remained totally disconnected from them. I was reminded of a caged animal, one that had been roughly treated for a long time, and had learned simply to await the abuses its owners chose to mete out.

While we watched, Craig's hand crept out, and quickly opened the oven on the toy cooker, which was just above his head. He took something out, nibbled on it quickly, and then replaced it, all the time watching to see if anyone had seen him.

I looked over at Irma. 'A biscuit?'

'Yes. Come and look at this.'

She took me into the boys' bathroom. A potty, moulded in pink plastic into the shape of a pig, had been placed beside the toilet.

'Look down at the U-bend,' Irma said.

I squatted and peered round the bowl of the toilet. Sitting on the curve of the pipe was a stack of three chocolate-chip cookies, the top one partially eaten. Beside these was a small, red, toy car.

'He comes in here, sits on the pot, plays with the car and has a munch. We make sure, obviously, that the pipe gets a specially thorough scrub every day—not that we didn't always, anyway.'

'And where does he get the biscuits? Does he bring them in himself?'

'Lord, no. He never even has any lunch—we provide that for him and two other kids from similar backgrounds. We have milk and biscuits at eleven o'clock every day. A plate of biscuits is put out, and the children help themselves. It would appear Craig hasn't been eating all of his, though.'

I stood up. 'He's hoarding,' I said. 'And I'd bet it's not just here and the home corner.'

'No.' Irma nodded. 'There's a spot outside in the yard and another in the cloakroom. And it's not just biscuits, although they're his favourite. Sandwiches show up, too, and fruit. Whatever he's given, really.'

'Have you said anything to him about it?'

Irma sighed and put her hands in the pockets of her jeans. 'No. To be honest, I'm not altogether sure how much English he understands, so saying anything could well be pointless. But I sort of thought he'd grow out of this behaviour as he became more secure. He's been here two months now but he's still not mixing, and he continues to stockpile food. I'm not sure what to do.'

'Hoarding usually occurs where kids have suffered real hunger. They've had the experience of not knowing where the next meal is coming from, so they ensure that, in an emergency, they'll be ready. It's like taking out an insurance policy. D'you know anything about his home background?'

'His mother drops him off and picks him up, and, to be honest, she seems to have only a little more English than him. She's as frightened and nervy as Craig is. I'm guessing, but I don't think they come from any place good.'

I nodded. 'Two months is a long time for him to be still so cut off from the other kids. How do they respond to him?'

'They tried to engage with him in the early days when he first came. They'd go up and ask him if he wanted to play. He reacted violently initially: he hit and bit them, screamed at them in Romanian. Well, as you can imagine, they stopped making any effort fairly quickly after that, and it just slipped into the present status quo. He sits there on his own, and they ignore him.'

'I don't think that kind of isolation should continue. Have you thought about ways to get him more involved?'

'Oh, we've done more than thought about it. We've tried to get him involved in group games. We had a go at getting him to sing some songs. I went into that corner with some paints and paper, but it was no good. He just sat there, like a statue, then, when I looked away for a moment, he spilt the paint all over the floor.'

'Is he under weight? It's difficult to tell when he's in that position.'

'No. He was, but he's fattened up a little over the past two months. All the biscuits, maybe.'

I rubbed my beard and thought for a moment. 'I have an idea. I'll be back tomorrow. I think I might just be able to get Craig to open up a little.'

'And how do you propose to do that?' Irma asked.

I grinned. 'I need to get some things together; just bear with me.'

———

Craig looked at me with unveiled suspicion the following day when I arrived. I took off my coat and, with some art materials, went over and sat opposite him in his corner. I said nothing for a few moments as I spread out the paper, pencils and crayons, and then, when they were all arrayed before him, I smiled.

'*Salut*,' I said.

Craig looked at me with deep puzzlement. I tried again: '*Ce mai fac?*' This is Romanian for 'How are you?'

Craig's mouth dropped open. '*Mulțumesc, bine*,' he said, at last, almost so quietly I couldn't hear—'Fine, thank you.'

'*Cum te cheamă?*' I asked—'What is your name?'

'*Numele meu e* Litovoi,' the child replied—'My name is *Litovoi*.' There was a pause, then: '*Nu* Craig.'—'Not *Craig*.'

I extended my hand. '*Îmi pare bine*, Litovoi. *Numele meu e* Shane.'—'It's nice to meet you, Litovoi. My name is Shane.'

Don't get the wrong idea—I'm terrible at languages, and my Romanian is not even functional. Before that day, I had no Romanian at all, despite the fact that I had worked with several Romanian families. They had all spoken English, so I had seen no reason to bother. But it occurred to me that the language barrier may have been a starting point for Craig's—Litovoi's—isolation. Of course, if he was to settle into his life in Ireland, he would need to learn English. But was it too much to expect that the childcare workers in the place he spent the most time during the week might learn a few words of Romanian, his first language, to help him with the transition? So I had gone online, and found a site that provided me with some key phrases. The website contained a phonetic pronunciation of each, which meant I could rehearse what I meant to say.

Romanian is actually a language that lends itself quite well to phonetics, but I knew there were sounds that native speakers used—clicks and pops and things—that I would never even be able to attempt. But I was determined to have a go at communicating. I had hoped that speaking to this frightened, lonely child in the tongue of his homeland might elicit a reaction.

I was not surprised at the child's aversion to his new name. Many Eastern European, African and Asian immigrants realise that the very pronunciation of their names can be a barrier to integration. Irish people and, as I've said, I'm no exception, are not good at learning other languages, and the effort of getting their mouths round strange-sounding words can sometimes, ludicrously, seem just too much bother. Therefore, often with no real disrespect meant, they will shorten foreign names to make life easier for themselves. Vladislav becomes Vic. Petrovich becomes Pete. Litovoi, with no easy English shortening, became Craig. Over time, it seemed that a lot of families decided to get in there first and change their own and their children's names, before the general public did it for them. I never found out whether Craig was a label given to Litovoi by a well-meaning Irish person, or if his parents had re-christened him. In the end, it didn't matter. He knew it wasn't his name.

In my halting, atrociously pronounced Romanian, I told Litovoi that I did not know much of his language, but I thought he looked lonely and I wanted to chat to him. He listened intently, his eyes huge and blue and still full of suspicion and doubt.

'*Român dus?*' he asked when I had stumbled through my short speech—'Are you Romanian?'

'*Irlandez,*' I said, patting my chest.

That seemed to be the end of things, as far as he was concerned. He looked away, holding his knees even more tightly. I had expected this, and pulled over the art materials. 'Litovoi,' I said, '*iată nite jucării.*'—'Here are some things to play with.'

He glanced at the paper and crayons, and I saw him flicker. He wanted to play with them, but he had become so entrenched in his remoteness that he had almost forgotten how to. I picked up a blue crayon, and drew a group of matchstick figures in one corner of the page, all of them with smiling faces. Then, in the opposite corner, I drew, in black, a much smaller figure, in an almost foetal position. I picked the page up and dropped it on his knees, directly under his nose.

His eyes remained directed at the wall. I had ceased to exist for him—I was the enemy.

'Litovoi,' I said, tapping the page. '*Acel dus.*'—'That's you.'

No response. I smiled to myself. At barely three years old, this little boy had a remarkable amount of inner fortitude. I drew another picture and put it on top of the first one. This was an image of a crayon, then a simple picture of a boy drawing with it. Then, beside that, a picture of a chocolate-chip cookie. Litovoi's eyes flicked downwards for a second. I took an actual cookie from my pocket and held it out to him.

'*Eu am mai mult,*' I said—'I have more.'

'*Mult?*' he asked tentatively.

I nodded, and pushed the paper over to him. He took a bite from the biscuit, and then moved to put the remainder in his pocket. 'Hey,' I said, and produced the bag I had in *my* pocket. He stopped midway. '*Dus nu avepei nevoie de la,*' I said—'You don't need to.' I was aware that my diction was appalling (how he had thought, even for a moment, that I was Romanian, I'll never know), but I wanted him to see that he didn't have to worry about where the next one was coming from, that there was no need to hoard. I took another one out of the bag, and bit off half of it, chewed quickly, then swallowed the rest. '*A vedea?*'—'See?'

A smile spread across his face, and he put the rest of the biscuit into his mouth in one go, crunching merrily.

'Chocolate-chip cookie,' he said suddenly.

Now it was my turn to look at him, aghast.

'Yes! Chocolate-chip cookie! *Cipul de ciocolată* cookie!'

Litovoi started to laugh. He had a deep-throated, full-bodied chuckle that was infectious and, before I knew it, I was laughing too. All the heads in the room twisted in our direction. Some of the children giggled. It seemed that Litovoi's laughter was a new sound to staff and children alike.

I discovered, during the next hour, as Litovoi drew one picture after another, and chomped his way through most of the cookies, that his English was considerably better than my Romanian. We chatted in a kind of pidgin mixture of both languages, and gradually, through our talk and the images he drew, I began to understand just what was causing this little boy to remove himself in such a way.

———

Later that day, when the kids had all gone home, I sat over tea with Irma and Jean, another staff member, who was also Litovoi's key worker, meaning she had special responsibility for him.

'From what I can gather Petru Tomescu was either a soldier or a terrorist back in Romania,' I said. 'Litovoi draws him with a gun a lot. He refers to him as a *soldat*, which means, literally, soldier. So he could have been in the military. But then, an awful lot of the gangs refer to their members in military terms. It doesn't mean he was actually a member of the armed forces. Litovoi could be just mixed up.'

'I can't get used to calling him that,' Jean said. 'I mean, he's Craig, isn't he?'

'No, he's not,' I said. 'He's quite adamant that Craig isn't his name.'

'Weird,' Jean said, shaking her head.

'I don't know much about the political background of Romania,' I said, 'beyond the whole Ceauşescu thing. From what I can gather, they still have national service, and as an ex-communist state it would be natural there'd still be quite a bit of political unrest. Petru could have been involved in some kind of left-wing resistance, or simply a member of the Romanian mafia. They're very organised, or so I'm told.'

'Petru is well known as being involved in all sorts of things,' Irma said. 'So why does Craig hide away in the corner, then? I mean, his father being either a soldier or a criminal doesn't have to impact on him. Lots of children of gangsters have wonderful home lives, don't they?'

'The Tomescus have spent the past few years—Litovoi's entire life, really—moving around,' I said. 'He drew five different pictures of "home" for me—five different houses and flats. And he's only three! He couldn't have stayed in any one spot for more than a few months. That means he's never made friends he's been able to hold on to. His attitude now seems to be that there's just no point.'

'And he can speak English?'

'Yes. But not well, and he likes to have a bit of Romanian thrown in. It makes him feel safer, I think. Look, I'll print you out a sheet of basic phrases. They're not hard, I learned enough last night to be able to hold a reasonable conversation with him today. The other kids could learn some too—wouldn't do them any harm, and it'd help him to be accepted.'

'What about the hoarding?'

'That'll work itself out, in time, I reckon. The economic situation in Romania isn't great. But look, both parents are working now, so I'd recommend a conversation with Elvira. She should at least be providing the kid with a lunch. There's no reason for him to go hungry now. He seems clean, and although his clothes are old, they're quite adequate. The family could simply have got into a rut.'

'I'll try,' Jean said. 'But she just comes in and takes him. We've tried to talk to her before, but she always looks frightened and runs off.'

'She must have some level of English—why don't you try a few key words in Romanian? It couldn't hurt.'

The women looked sceptical, but agreed. I left that afternoon, believing I'd heard the last of the Tomescus. I was wrong.

Chapter 2 ∽

I worked for an organisation called the Dunleavy Trust, a voluntary group that specialises in helping children that no one else could. The young people on our books were all in states of crisis, and the professionals working with them had usually exhausted their respective abilities and were at their wits' end.

Litovoi was not indicative of the types of case I usually handled. He was having difficulty settling into his crèche, but in all other respects he appeared to be in good health and was reasonably well looked after. But he was a sign of what was to come, not just in my own career, but for the entire Irish childcare profession.

The real problem lay not with the little boy, but in the fact that the women who worked with him had no idea of how to cope with a child from a Romanian background. While such kids had all the developmental needs of children everywhere, they presented challenges that were unique to their cultural group—a language barrier, a history of poverty and civil unrest and very often a childhood spent largely on the move.

Ireland had experienced a huge influx of families from diverse ethnic backgrounds in a very short space of time. Since the beginnings of the Celtic Tiger boom in the mid-1990s, a steady flow of migrants, mostly from Eastern Europe and the poorer parts of Africa, had poured across our borders looking for work and a life free from poverty and oppression. They expected to find streets lined with golden euro coins and the hundred thousand welcomes the Irish are famous for the world over.

Unfortunately, while they certainly found ready work, the welcome was a little colder than they had expected. Irish people were just not ready for such a vast change. Within the space of twelve months Ireland went from mono- to multi-cultural. The government looked on, secretly delighted but oblivious to the social time bomb that was being created.

The Irish economy had been in drastic danger of overheating. There weren't enough workers to do all the low-paid, though very important, jobs that needed to be carried out to keep the community functioning. These new arrivals represented a huge workforce and they immediately applied themselves to these lowly tasks, taking up posts in factories, the hospitality industry, in construction and in many other areas that were having difficulty sourcing staff.

But the process of integrating such a large number of ethnic minorities—it has been reckoned in recently published statistics that the Polish residents of Ireland alone make up approximately 10 per cent of the entire population—was never really begun. Eastern European migrants in particular became rapidly ghettoised, moving into flats and tenements in the slums of Irish towns and cities, and keeping themselves to themselves. They generally steered clear of pubs and cafés, socialising in one another's apartments or houses.

Many of the native population remained deeply wary of their new neighbours. These Nigerians, Poles, Romanians and Kosovans had been through experiences, had lived through hardships that our ancestors might have understood but which were totally alien to the soft, well-fed modern Irish consciousness. They had grown up in cultures where the phrase 'survival of the fittest' was not just an empty concept but a way of life. Here were people who knew what it was like to starve, who had been hunted and persecuted, who had survived under ideologies where women were forced to submit to mutilation and barbarity. On the face of it, the Irish should have had a good deal in common with the new arrivals. We had a cultural memory of being colonised, a communal recollection of poverty, which should have made us empathise with the disadvantaged. Yet we had, in the main, overcome such adversities and were experiencing the first bloom of a time of plenty: we were uncomfortable with sharing it.

To be honest, at this stage in my career, I had little experience of working with anything other than Irish children. I had encountered one or two Romanian kids, and I was aware that more and more children from other ethnic groups were being taken into residential care. I knew there were a huge number of foreign children on the missing persons lists, but this had, as yet, barely impacted on me. It was as if the non-national community was one Ireland, and the world I lived in was another.

These two realities became superimposed for the first time one day as I sat at the desk in my untidy office, reading a case file that had just been handed to me at the team meeting earlier that morning. My phone rang.

It was Beverly Munro, the Trust's secretary and receptionist. Actually she was much more than that. My boss, Ben Tyrrell, often referred to her as 'the keeper of the flame'. She knew every single one of the families we worked with, could remember dates of appointments that were to happen months into the future, and even the details of minutes of meetings she had kept several years ago. She could immediately call to mind the telephone number and email address of every social worker, psychologist, speech therapist or youth worker we dealt with, and could tell you exactly what role they played in whichever case they were involved in. The problem is, there isn't really a title that comes close to describing everything she did. Perhaps 'keeper of the flame' captured her best.

'Shane,' Mrs Munro said, 'I have a lady at reception who is asking to see you. Her name is Elvira Tomescu. She won't tell me what it is in relation to.'

I closed the file and sat back, puzzled. It took me a moment to remember where I had heard the name before. 'Could you send her into the meeting room, Mrs Munro? I'll be with her in a moment.'

Elvira Tomescu was probably not much more than twenty-five. She had the slightly tanned, sallow look many Romanians have, and her hair was the same colour as her son's, a sort of tawny light brown. She was slim, and when she stood up at the end of our meeting, I saw that she was as tall as I was. She was pretty in a tired, careworn way. She wore an anorak that was a little too large for her over the uniform of a chambermaid from one of the large hotel chains.

'You see my son, Craig,' she said, the moment I came through the door of the meeting room.

'Mrs Tomescu, my name is Shane Dunphy,' I said, extending my hand. She shook it limply. 'Yes, I was asked to meet your son, Litovoi, at his pre-school, because he was finding it difficult to settle and make friends with the other children. I had a chat with him, and, as I haven't heard from the staff there for two weeks, I expect he's doing quite well, now. You should be pleased.'

'His name is Craig.'

'That's not what he told me.'

'*Litovoi* is no good. People here, they no say that name. Craig easy. You tell them, he is Craig.'

I sighed. Why was nothing simple?

'Mrs Tomescu, your son is entitled to his name. I bet if I rang Irma right now, she'd tell me the other children are having no difficulty in pronouncing Litovoi.'

'You say he no have lunch.' She looked hurt, indignant and haughty. There was a fierce pride in this woman. I knew it had taken a great deal of courage for her to come here, and I admired her for it. I was not going to pretend, however, that everything was all right just to spare her feelings. Litovoi deserved better than that.

'He doesn't bring a lunch to pre-school, Mrs Tomescu. The

staff there provide him with one. He hides food in different places around the room because he is afraid that, one day, he'll have none. I know your family have probably had tough times, but things are different now. You can help him to learn that he doesn't need to save up his food any more by making sure he has a good lunch to take in every day. Does he get breakfast before he leaves the house?'

'We have no time.'

'Get up a little earlier, then. I don't want to sound insensitive, but that's all there is to it. Food is massively important to children. Their entire sense of security is wrapped up in it. Not getting enough to eat makes them feel terribly unsafe, and can have a knock-on effect on everything else. A hungry child won't try to socialise, won't learn properly, won't even grow normally. If you want your son to be accepted, Mrs Tomescu, you need to do this.'

I could sense her discomfort now. She seemed to jiggle up and down on her chair, as if she was about to bolt. 'He is bad boy. He will not get out of his bed.'

I felt sorry for her, but wasn't going to let her off the hook. 'Don't tell me that. He's three years old. He's out of bed in the morning before you are, unless you have him up half the night, in which case you need to put him to bed at a reasonable time, to make sure he can get up in time to have breakfast.'

She gave me a hard look. I don't know what she expected, coming to confront me like this. Whatever it was, though, she wasn't getting it.

'Look, Mrs Tomescu,' I said, trying to soften my voice, 'Litovoi is a wonderful little boy. He's clever and friendly and he wants to learn. It's just that he's had some tough experiences for a boy of his age. You and your husband are working, isn't that right?'

'Yes, we work hard.'

'Good. That means you have enough money to give your son a healthy, packed lunch every day, and to make sure he has a good breakfast every morning. That will make a big difference to how he feels about himself. He's still adjusting to a new place, and it's even harder because no one really speaks his first language; he probably feels quite lonely.'

'He must learn English.'

'Yes, he must,' I agreed, 'and he will. He already knows quite a bit.'

'You tell women to speak Romanian. No good! No good speak to him like that.'

'I asked the staff at the pre-school to try a few words of Romanian to make Litovoi feel more secure. And he did. You want him to be happy, don't you?'

Suddenly Elvira's eyes filled with tears. It was as though someone had switched on a tap, so sudden was it.

'Yes,' she said, and nodded vigorously, the tears streaming down her cheeks. 'I want him be happy. He my son.'

I reached over and took her hand, which she didn't pull away. 'Hey, that's okay, Mrs Tomescu. I know you want what's best for him. Look, this all sounds awful at the moment, but it's not really. I can help you, and so can Irma and Jean at the crèche. If you're really struggling—with money, I mean—the pre-school can continue providing lunches for a while. I can call to your home, if you like, if you're having problems getting Litovoi to bed. There are ways of managing difficult behaviour. Kids don't come with instructions and sometimes parents can feel very isolated.'

I might as well have slapped her. 'No! No one comes to my house. Please.' She wrenched her hand back, and all the blood ran from her face. 'You cannot come.' She was visibly trembling.

'Okay, that's not a problem,' I said, a little puzzled. 'I just want you to realise that there are people to help if you're having problems. There's no shame in running into difficulties. The shame is when you don't accept help if you need it.'

The woman was still obviously shaken. She seemed terrified, all of a sudden. 'We no need help. I will give him lunch. He will get breakfast. I will prepare these things for him. He will be fine. He is a good boy. You will see.'

At that, she stood up and, without another word, bolted from the room. I heard Mrs Munro say something, and then the front door slammed. I stood up, and went into the kitchen to get some more coffee. I heard footsteps behind me.

'What did you say to her?' It was the keeper of the flame.

'I wish I knew. Did she mention anything as she rushed past?'

'Not a word. But she looked like all the hounds of hell were after her. Perhaps you need to work on your people skills.'

I shrugged and went back to my file. But I couldn't concentrate on it. Something wasn't right about my meeting with Litovoi's mother. Finally, I put the folder aside, and went to look for some answers.

Chapter 3 ∾

I sat on a bench in University Square, smoking a cigarette and watching the students come and go. They were all dressed as if there had been a going out of business sale at the local Oxfam shop. One tall thin kid wandered past me carrying a pile of books, an acoustic guitar slung over his shoulder. Along with a faded tracksuit top, Converse trainers and baggy jeans, he had on what looked like a Davy Crockett style 'coon-skin cap. Ireland wasn't exactly overrun with racoons, so I assumed he must have bought it somewhere. It was a sunny day, and far too warm for such pioneering headgear. But, then, he looked cool—or something.

'Shane!'

The person I had come to meet waved at me from the arched gateway of the college. Cedric Wallis could have passed for a student himself, albeit a mature one. His long dark hair, shot through with grey, was tied back in a loose ponytail. His beard was also long but wispy, and he wore bell-bottomed jeans and a hoodie made of some kind of natural, undyed wool. His feet were shod in what looked like straw sandals. Standing alongside him, I felt particularly neat and tidy, which is a rare feeling for me.

Cedric had taught me sociology during my student days, and was probably the most ridiculously intelligent human being I have ever met. He is also one of the few Irish sociologists who is unafraid to get his hands dirty and still engages in real social research, actually leaving his study to get out and meet people. You are as likely to find Cedric Wallis hanging out with street gangs in Ballymun as you are to encounter him giving a high-minded lecture to a conference of professors. To his credit, he is equally at home doing both.

'Hey, it's great to see you,' Cedric said, grinning. 'There's a fab vegetarian restaurant across the square. You promised to buy me lunch, I believe.'

We got seats at the window, so I could continue my people-watching. The menus came on recycled paper. Most of the dishes listed contained the words 'organic', 'wholegrain' or 'free range'.

'Talk to me about the non-national community,' I said as we both perused the lunch options.

'How long have you got?' Cedric laughed. 'That's like asking me to tell you about, I dunno, trees. There are thousands of different types, all with different colours and textures and patterns of growth.'

'Fair point. I'm working with a Romanian kid at the moment,' I said. 'And I just had a bizarre meeting with his mother.' I told Cedric what had happened. 'So what do you think?'

A waitress took our orders and left a jug of iced water.

'I think,' Cedric said, as he poured some into each of our glasses, 'that you were spectacularly insensitive, Shane.'

'Oh,' I said, more than a little taken aback. 'Well, shit, Cedric. Don't hold back now, tell me what you really think.'

'Don't get precious; you asked me,' he said. 'You went into the meeting with her carrying a raft of useless assumptions based on racial stereotypes, and, to be honest, a naive belief in how the system works. I'm surprised at you. Didn't I teach you anything?'

'Okay, rewind for a minute,' I said, feeling hurt despite myself. 'Let's go back to the racial stereotypes.'

'Has it occurred to you that her insistence on the boy speaking English might be more than just some misplaced notion about speeding up his integration?'

'What?'

'And the same goes for changing his name. It's easy for you to plough in with your noble concepts of personal and cultural pride, but the reality is that such things are often too dangerous to entertain. Patriotism is an ideal that few people can actually afford.'

'I still don't follow.'

'Let's start on a bureaucratic level. Have you seen the paperwork on the Tomescus? Their work visas, applications for refugee status, even their passports?'

'No. I wouldn't generally have access to that kind of material.'

'Mmmm. It would be quite interesting to see if the name "Litovoi" appears on those forms.'

'Why wouldn't it?'

'A huge number of the non-nationals who are working in Ireland are here with false papers. I've encountered individuals through my research who have half a dozen different aliases.'

'Yeah, the adults, maybe, but their children?'

'You've suggested to me that the father, Petru, may have been involved in organised crime?'

'Yeah, but that's purely a hunch. Nothing has been pinned on him yet. Some of the things Litovoi said would hint at it, though.'

'Consider this: the family in question have been on the move around mainland Europe for several years, never staying in one place for very long. They arrive in Ireland off the boat—much less security there, wouldn't you say? If you're a foot passenger, you wave your passport and you're through. Isn't it feasible that the Tomescus are running away from something?'

'Aren't all the immigrants here running from something, Cedric? Poverty, war, unemployment?'

'Possibly, but they don't traipse around the entire bloody Continent before coming here, do they?'

'No, I s'pose not.'

'And, anyway, how do you know for certain that they *did* travel round Europe?'

'Litovoi told me.'

'A three-year-old child told you he spent twelve months

trotting about various European countries?'

'Not in so many words ...'

'I mean,' Cedric was on a roll now, his eyes bright and his hands gesticulating wildly as he worked through various theories, 'they could have spent time going from one place to another within the accession states, and then come here via Liverpool.'

'Possibly.'

'I have to tell you, it's more likely.'

'How so?'

'You've heard of the Red Mafiya?'

'Sure.'

'Well, they're the largest of a hugely intricate network of criminal gangs who operate in that part of the world. Since the fall of communism in what was called the Eastern Bloc, they have more or less come to dominate life on a local and national scale in that part of the globe. They trade in drugs, money laundering, protection, illegal boxing, numbers, but guess what their biggest earner is?'

'What?'

'People trafficking.' Cedric sat back as the waitress brought our food. 'There is a long line,' he continued, 'of people wanting to get into the West. Ireland isn't alone in being a destination for refugees, you know. Spain, France, Germany, the United Kingdom, all of them have problems controlling immigration. But at least the other countries I've named are used to it. They've all had forty years to come to grips with the complexities of the issue. Here, we acknowledge that there are gaping holes in our legislation and practices, but that's about as far as it goes. Nothing has been done.'

'And how does that relate to the Tomescus?'

'Well, an admirable reason for your Elvira to be so upset at her son revealing his real name to an interfering busybody, is that the name on his passport does not match up—because that passport is a fake.'

'You're suggesting they were trafficked in illegally.'

'I am. It all adds up. Petru, which almost certainly isn't his real name, was probably involved in crime in Romania. He either fell out with his gang, or possibly offended another group of criminals. He may even have drawn the attention of the police to himself. Either way, he and his family had to leave the country quickly. The best way would have been to go to one of the many traffickers. Petru would've known several, through his connections. Their movements, which the boy has alluded to, could well have taken place as they sourced the various papers and documents necessary for the journey. They may also have had to go into hiding if Petru was in bad odour with a particular gang. Slights, insults or betrayals are responded to with violence. Usually of the terminal kind.'

I nodded. About us, the restaurant was filling up, mostly with students and lecturers. It was a testimony to the grip of the economic boom Ireland was experiencing that students could afford to eat in a place like this. During my college days, such luxuries would have been unthinkable.

'I thought trafficking only involved the movement of people who didn't really want to be moved,' I said, after we'd eaten in silence for a few moments. 'It's a major part of the slave trade, isn't it?'

'There are many different levels of the slave trade, and just as many ways of sucking people into it. Let's assume Petru approached a gangster, as I suggest. He needs new identities for himself and his family. He wishes to go somewhere they won't be known and where he'll be fairly sure to get a job. That means counterfeit passports, plane or boat tickets and a contact at landfall.'

'All quite pricey, I'd imagine.'

'Yes. It varies, of course, but in general, you'll pay anywhere from one thousand to fifteen hundred euro to get out of one of the Eastern European states and into Ireland.'

'And if you don't have that kind of money?'

'Well, that's the really interesting part.' Cedric grinned, sucking up a strand of spaghetti. 'People who can't afford to get false papers made up can try to stow away on board ships, or get brought over in the boots of cars, but that sort of thing is uncomfortable and unreliable, not to mention dangerous. So many families agree to work off the amount when they get here. The agents responsible for bringing them from Poland, or Latvia or wherever—who are, more often than not, also their landlords—come round on a weekly basis, and take as much as three quarters of their wages for rent, debt repayments, and sometimes ludicrous fictitious taxes they've just invented.'

'You're not serious.'

'I'm deadly serious. The interest on the loans—the "vig", I've heard it called—is just abominable, and a hell of a lot of the poor buggers caught up in these scams never manage to pay them off. They just get sucked in deeper and deeper.'

'So, despite the fact that Petru and Elvira are both working,' I said, realisation dawning, 'they may, quite feasibly, be unable to afford to provide Litovoi with lunch.'

'Exactly. You know, I've heard of quite a number of employers who actually take these payments directly out of workers' wages, and pay them into bank accounts. The system has become that formalised. And, of course, not all the gangs operating these scams are Eastern European. Many Irish criminals have gotten in on the act.'

'But this is the kind of thing you'd expect in Chicago during the prohibition era,' I spluttered. 'It can't be allowed to continue. I mean, it's all illegal, isn't it?'

'Oh, completely.' Cedric nodded. 'But you have to check in your principles at the door, Shane. This is a highly organised, very profitable business. These guys know exactly what they're doing. And you'd have to prove that the monies were being taken illegally. Adults can hand money over to whomever they wish, after all.'

'But it's crippling them financially!'

'Petru would have understood when he went to the trafficker in the first place, what he was getting into. Chances are he was involved at the criminal end of it himself before things went bad for him. The gangs see these people as a cash crop, and they are determined to harvest as much as they possibly can.'

'So how can I help them?'

Cedric shook his head. 'You can't. This is an institutional problem. It goes deep. The government is fully aware of the degree of exploitation that's going on. I'm not saying they *want* it to continue, but they're not exactly bending over backwards to prevent it either. Our economy needs the workforce the immigrants provide. And it's not just the powers that be, either. We're all abusing these poor people, every single one of us. I mean, you see that waitress over there?'

I looked. He was motioning at a pretty blonde girl who was carrying a stack of plates towards the kitchen. 'Yeah.'

'She's a fully qualified junior doctor.'

'Why is she working as a waitress, then?'

'Because she trained in the Ukraine her qualifications aren't fully recognised in Ireland. She'd have to spend a year doing another course before she'd be allowed to work here.'

'Wouldn't it be worth it to spend a year studying?'

'She has two sisters and a mother back home. Her mother is ill, and her sisters are training to be nurses. They depend on her. She sends them money, and from the rest of her wages she pays off her debt to the gangs. She can't afford to stop working to do a course.'

'But wouldn't she earn so much more as a doctor?'

'The obligations she has won't wait a year.'

I watched the girl; her cheeks were flushed and a thin sheen of sweat coated her forehead as she hurried about, wiping down tables and gathering up more dirty crockery. The food suddenly didn't seem so appetising.

'Look,' I said, pushing my unfinished meal away, 'I'm not trying to overturn the system, as crooked as it may be. My only concern is the child. I mean, why wouldn't Elvira want me calling over? I'm trying to help.'

Cedric shook his head. 'You're not listening to me, Shane. You may work in the voluntary sector, but to Elvira you *represent* the system. You are part of everything she wants to avoid. Your visiting her home has the capacity to bring God knows how many more professionals sniffing round her family. By simply talking to their son, you managed to find out his real name, and because you have now insisted he be addressed by it, you could have put the entire family at risk. Remember, there may be some very bad men looking for the Tomescus. They wouldn't be beyond using the child to get to the parents.'

I saw immediately that he was right, but it was hard to accept. 'I'd be careful. I could try to explain—'

'She won't care!' Cedric said, his voice urgent. 'You cannot even begin to comprehend what people like her have been through. Her world view is so far removed from yours, it's almost as though she's from a different planet. You need to rethink this, Shane.'

I glanced out the window for a moment. Across the square, an obviously foreign woman, a colourful headscarf covering her hair, was begging. I suddenly felt way out of my depth.

'So I can do nothing? Is that what you're saying?'

Cedric ordered an espresso from a passing waitress, and turned back to me. 'Is it possible that you need to think about "help" in a slightly different way?'

I was puzzled by that. 'What do you mean?'

He told me, and the seed of a plan took root.

Chapter 4 ∾

The file was still sitting on my desk when I got back to the office, and it didn't look any more inviting. I busied myself by tidying up my work area, making a few phone calls that would aid me in my new plan for the Tomescus, and then killed half an hour by joining Marian, a colleague who had popped in to pick up a report before going to court, for a cup of coffee. I probably made her even more late than she already was, but it was better than wading through the file.

Finally, around four o'clock that afternoon, there was no help for it, and I begrudgingly sat down and reopened the heavy folder. The subject of the file was an eleven-year-old boy named Edgar O'Sullivan. A photo clipped to the inside cover showed a dark-haired, freckled boy, chubby bordering on fat. He wore a puzzled expression, not smiling, but not exactly scowling at the camera either.

The case was fairly standard. Young Edgar was in a residential childcare unit in the city. He had been in care since he was six years old, as a result of appalling neglect at the hands of his mother. No one seemed to know who his father was, and that section of his birth certificate remained blank. Over the five years since his move into care, the boy's behaviour had become progressively more and more challenging. As I flipped through the pages, I saw that Edgar was very close to being expelled from his school—he had already been suspended twice that year. And things weren't much better for him at the unit. My eyes fell on a letter, written by the residence's manager to the residential co-ordinator, the person in charge of all residential services in the city. 'I must stress that Edgar has become wholly unsuitable for continued placement within our facility,' the letter concluded. 'His behaviour is that of a child experiencing severe trauma, and I feel that a period in high support may be beneficial for him. At any rate, I appeal to you to find alternative accommodation for this child as soon as possible. He is disrupting the lives of the seven other children at our unit, appears to harbour a deep antagonism towards all the staff members, and must be extremely unhappy.' The letter was dated from the previous week, and was signed by one Hugh Whitty.

I flicked through the remaining pages, not really taking much more in, until I came across a brief report on an access visit between Edgar and his mother, Collette. The report didn't tell me much, it was simply a list of what the pair had done for the two hours they'd been together (had coffee and buns at a café and then shopped for toys). What interested me was the name of the worker who had supervised the access visit.

Melanie Moorehouse was an ex-colleague of mine. We had met several years before, when I had been a community childcare worker for the Health Service Executive in a rural area. She and I had not hit it off very well initially, but had gradually become friends. She was a strong-willed, garrulous woman, and it seemed that she was now working for the HSE in the city, and was involved in Edgar's case. I picked up the phone.

'Shane Dunphy, how the fuck are you?' Melanie's voice bellowed down the receiver.

'I'm good, Melanie,' I said, smiling to myself. 'I'm going to be doing some work with a youngster you've got on your caseload. Edgar O'Sullivan.'

'You've landed that one, huh?'

'Yup.'

'It's a toughie.'

'Care to tell me about it?'

'Hang on a minute.' I could hear papers shuffling and muffled voices. 'You still there?' she asked a moment later.

'Yeah, I'm here.'

'Listen, I have to pop out for a bit. D'you want to meet up for a drink later, and I'll tell you all about our boy? I've got a few visits to make, won't be finished until around eight. I'll be just about ready for something containing a lot of alcohol by then.'

I laughed. 'I can do that. Where?'

She told me, and I hung up. I sat back, watching the light grow dim outside my window. A song thrush was perched on the branch of a tree in the overgrown garden at the rear of Dunleavy House which my office looked out on. The bird was singing for all it was worth, bidding the day farewell as if its life depended on it. I listened for a time, as the shadows got longer. The song was sad and beautiful and made me feel lonely and old, so I got up and went home for a while.

———

Melanie Moorehouse was taller than me, thirty-two years old, and looked as though she worked out and watched what she ate. Her dark hair was thick, long and caught the light when she moved. Her make-up was carefully applied and her clothes, which fitted her extremely well, were all perfectly colour co-ordinated and very much in fashion. Despite all this, she looked tired and stressed when she arrived into the city-centre bar at twenty-five past eight that evening.

She plonked down in the chair opposite me, and grinned. 'Hey, you,' she said, and leaned over to give me a kiss.

'Hello, Melanie,' I said.

'Sorry I'm late.'

'I expected you to be. Want a drink?'

'Fuck, yeah. Bacardi and Coke. Large.'

I went to the bar and got her one.

'Have you eaten?' I asked as I sat down. 'They serve pub grub, I think.'

'Let me just dive into this first, okay?'

'Yeah, no problem.'

She took a long swallow of her drink, and lit a cigarette. 'You're with the Dunleavy Trust now,' she said.

'Yup. For my sins.'

'How'd you land that?'

'They came looking for me, actually.'

'Do you like it?'

I shrugged. 'Sometimes. You're still with the HSE.'

'It's permanent. It's pensionable. That's hard to walk away from these days.'

'Do *you* like it?'

She smiled at me over the rim of her glass. 'Sometimes.'

I laughed. 'This strange thing we do.'

'Yet we still do it.'

I lit a cigarette of my own. 'Maybe it's better than a real job.'

Melanie drained her Bacardi. She had consumed the beverage in three swallows. 'I don't think I can remember what a real job is.'

I got us both fresh drinks, and we ordered some food. When it arrived, I turned the conversation to Edgar.

'He's not an easy kid to sum up,' Melanie said after a long pause. 'You know how there are some clients who have a huge effect on you? Those children who are still on your mind long after you clock off? The ones you wake up in the middle of the night thinking about, worrying about?'

'Yeah, we all have them.'

Melanie nibbled on a crisp. 'Edgar is sort of like that for me, only for all the wrong reasons.'

I shook my head. 'I don't follow.'

My companion sighed and had another taste of her drink. 'Remember when you got into childcare initially? How we all wanted to save the world? I know I thought every child was special.'

'Of course,' I agreed. 'I mean, who doesn't feel like that in the beginning? When you're starting out, and full of passion for the work, there's not a social ill that can't be cured.'

'Right.' Melanie had a distant look as she recalled those first exciting days in her chosen profession. 'And you can see the best in every kid, even the really tough ones. You make the effort to look super hard, and, usually, you find a way to get through all the bluster and bravado, and find the sweet innocent child underneath it all.'

'Yeah, I remember being like that,' I said, smiling at the recollection. 'I suppose, in a way, I'm still a little bit like it. Hell, so are you. It's part of the job description, isn't it?'

Melanie shook her head. 'Have you ever met a kid you just couldn't find the good in?'

And I suddenly realised why she seemed so upset.

Child protection workers are human beings. Even if robots could be designed to do what we do, I doubt they'd be much good at it, because emotion is at the core of every interaction, and the primary tools we work with are the relationships we establish with the children.

This means that such relationships need to be psychodynamic: there has to be a two-way flow. As a therapeutic worker, you give something to the child you are working with: friendship, security, advice and time. The child, however, gives something back. Often this will involve venting some very negative emotions. It is hugely important that the childcare worker is aware of how that symbiosis is making him or her feel. We are, of course, trained to deal with negative feelings, and ninety-nine times out of a hundred, we get so much positive stuff as well, it cancels the bad elements out.

But there is always that one case that just seems to grate on you. A child who, for whatever reason, doesn't gel. No matter what you try, regardless of all the little tricks of the trade you've picked up along the way, nothing works, and months later, you are still at stage one. Maybe you've even gone backwards. These are the children who are the most difficult to like.

Of course, no two clients are the same. Some are blissfully easy. Those kids we take to our hearts immediately; others require a little more time. The worker slowly, painstakingly constructs an emotional space where he and the child can meet and gradually bond.

Sometimes, though, for reasons that are not always obvious, we encounter a child with whom none of this works. And the natural, human response is to rebel against such a child. Our professional skills are insulted. The years of experience, all the successes, the countless families we have helped, are all diminished by this one loveless little boy or girl who will not respond to our overtures.

I could tell that Melanie was agonising over just such a case, and didn't want anything I said to aggravate things even more.

'Mel,' I began, taking a deep breath, 'the kids we work with are people, just the same as any others. Some you click with, others you don't. That's just the way life is.'

'But aren't we supposed to be better than that?' she asked. Her eyes had begun to get that misty look that usually precedes tears. That shocked me—the Melanie I knew didn't cry easily.

'No! I don't think we are,' I said, reaching over and taking her hand. 'You see, I've always believed that our job was about being truthful to ourselves about how we felt. You just *can't* like every kid or every family you encounter. The trick is to treat them all the same way, regardless.'

'Unconditional positive regard,' Melanie said, tears streaming down her cheeks. She was referring to a concept developed by the great therapist Carl Rogers which is kind of a mantra for social-care workers. It means that, no matter what a client has done, no matter how they treat you, you always deal with them with absolute respect and warmth. In many ways, it is the toughest part of the job, but it is absolutely essential.

'Exactly,' I said. 'You might not like Edgar, but as long as he feels safe and nurtured when he's with you, it doesn't matter. How you feel is really important, but the crucial thing is how *you're* making *him* feel.'

Melanie nodded, and squeezed my hand. 'I know, and I understand that. It's just that, truthfully, I feel like a fucking shit, you know? I dread seeing the little darling. Sometimes I think I actually decide before every access visit that I'm going to have a rotten time. What do you call it, a self-fulfilling prophecy? And I wonder if he's picking up on that.'

'Do you think he is?'

She laughed bitterly. 'Well, Shaney boy, that's kind of the crux of the thing. I don't know. Edgar O'Sullivan is a closed book, not just to me, but to the staff at his unit, to the teachers at his school—to himself, even, I reckon.'

'How long have you been working with him?'

'I've been supervising access visits between him and his awful fucking goblin of a mother for a year now.'

'And in all that time, you haven't gotten to know him at all?'

'Not even slightly. It's like ... like he's just not there. There's nothing behind his eyes. Sometimes I think he's dead inside. It's impossible to explain. You need to meet him yourself.'

'I will, tomorrow.'

Melanie raised her glass in a toast. 'To Edgar,' she said. 'May you have more luck with him than I've had.'

'I hope so.'

She fumbled about in her handbag, and produced a pack of tissues.

'Want to get drunk?' she asked, as she wiped her eyes.

'I've got an early start in the morning.'

'Me too. What's that got to do with anything?'

I couldn't think of an argument. 'Okay, then. It's your round.'

'Fucking A,' Melanie said, and stood up. She stopped for a moment and stared down at me. I was struck by how beautiful she looked, just then, and how terribly sad. 'Thanks for ... well ... for listening to all that crap.'

'No worries. We all have our moments, Mel. Comes with the territory.'

She sniffed and rubbed at her eyes again with the tissue. 'I'm glad you're on the case. I think he could do with some fresh energy, that kid—he needs someone to like him. It must be tough being surrounded by all these people who just fucking tolerate you.'

'I'll do my best. I can't promise any more than that.'

She nodded and went to get our drinks. I only have a vague recollection of getting home.

Chapter 5 ⌇

I awoke the following morning, and wished I hadn't.
The room seemed to have adopted a lurching, bobbing
motion it didn't usually have, and for the first half hour of
consciousness I had to hold on to the mattress to prevent myself
from falling off. Finally, I managed to make my way to the
bathroom, a trick I accomplished by grabbing every piece of
furniture en route.

A shower later, I felt somewhat revived, and managed to force
down a glass of orange juice and some dry toast. Sitting at the
breakfast table, I opened my diary and squinted at the scribbled
appointments. The entire morning had been blocked off for a
meeting with Hugh Whitty, the manager of Edgar O'Sullivan's
residential unit, followed by some time with young Edgar himself.
Moaning, I had two cups of black coffee, then delicately made my
way out to my ancient Austin, and drove across town.

———

The unit, which was called Bluecloud (a Native American name,
the manager later informed me), was a large, three-storey
townhouse, with a good-sized walled garden. It was a Wednesday,
so all the kids were at school—except for Edgar, who had been
expelled in the few days since his file had been updated.

The boy met me at the door, standing directly behind the staff
member who answered my ring. He was short for his age, and
looked much heavier than he did in his photo. He remained quite

motionless as I introduced myself, looking at me but not seeming to be taking anything in. I learned later that this was a misconception. Edgar took *everything* in.

'Hi, Edgar, I'm Shane,' I said to him. 'I'm going to be spending some time with you for the next while.' I held out my hand for him to shake.

The boy's eyes remained fixed on my face for what seemed like a minute, but was probably less. Finally he looked at my outstretched hand, and took it. Rather than shaking it, though, he somehow inverted his index finger and stroked my palm. It was an old schoolyard prank, but I wasn't prepared, and it made me shudder involuntarily. There was something sensual and singularly intrusive about the act—it was almost like an assault—and I pulled my hand away quickly.

Edgar didn't say a word throughout all this, just continued to eye me. I wondered if he was aware of the discomfort he had caused, but he gave no sign.

'Aren't you going to introduce yourself?' the female staff member asked him.

The boy eyed me some more, then shook his head and stomped away into the bowels of the house. I felt bile rising in my throat, and my head throbbed. The woman shook her head. 'He'll be stuck at home now until we find another school that'll take him. Fun, fun, fun.'

'I suppose getting expelled can't have done much for his self-esteem,' I offered.

'It'd take more than that to dent his armour,' she muttered, and brought me to Hugh Whitty's office.

Hugh was in his early forties, tall and thin, with a shock of grey hair fanning out from his head in corkscrew curls. His office was spacious, and was dominated by a wooden desk and two big, leather, swivel chairs. A very large print of Van Gogh's *Starry Night* adorned one of the walls, and was the first thing you saw on entering.

'Edgar is posing a real stumbling block for my team,' Hugh told me, without ceremony. 'He doesn't belong here, and I'm not too proud to tell you we don't have the skills to give him what he needs. I've been informed there isn't a bed available in high support right now, so we are, as they say, stuck with him. My supervisor suggested we place a call to your agency, so I did.'

'I've been over his file, and I had a ... er ... lengthy meeting with Melanie Moorehouse yesterday, but could you maybe give me your own perspective on him? I mean, you and your staff are with him day in, day out—you know him better than anyone else.'

Hugh looked down, seemingly abashed. 'Gee, it's cool of you to say so. A lot of social workers I deal with have a dim view of what we do in res.'

'I'm not a social worker, Hugh. I've served my time in residential, and I know exactly what it's like. Believe me, I have nothing but respect for what you do.'

'Wow, that's really decent of you.'

It struck me that Melanie was not the only person in contact with this boy who was having a crisis of confidence. I pushed the thought aside.

'So, fill me in on Edgar.'

Hugh sat back in his chair, and put his feet up on the desk. 'Edgar was a skinny, frightened little thing when he first came here. He'd experienced some of the worst neglect I've ever come across. He looked like something from a concentration camp. Just awful.'

'Did he ever speak about what his life was like at home?' I interjected. 'His mother has supervised access—have you had much contact with her? Is she receiving any therapy?'

'Edgar has never been forthcoming about his home life. His mother, Collette, would lead you to believe that their life was relatively idyllic. Any suggestion otherwise enrages her.'

'So she has no insight at all as to why her son is in care?'

Hugh spread his hands in a gesture of submission. 'Not so far as I can tell. But you see, she's not stupid. Far from it. I wouldn't be surprised if this is all part of some elaborate game she's playing.'

'It seems from the file that Edgar's behaviour has deteriorated over time. Do you think she may be partly responsible for that?'

'I certainly suspect so.'

'How has his behaviour changed?'

'Initially he was almost completely non-verbal. He refused to permit any of us to so much as touch him. He cowered any time someone came close, slept underneath his bed rather than in it, ate whatever was placed in front of him in a matter of seconds— he seemed to be terrified it would be taken away unless he devoured it as quickly as possible. He had never been toilet trained, so far as we could tell, and he wet and soiled himself incessantly. That was, I have to say, our first task—to house-break him, if you'll pardon the term.'

I waved away the phrase, although I didn't like the inference— 'house-break' seemed somehow disrespectful.

'Well, with no little difficulty, we managed to get him to use the facilities. As his time here progressed, he began to interact with us, but we always felt as if he was never truly opening up. There was a sense that he was simply giving us what he thought we wanted. Maybe a part of him needed us to open up to him too, but nobody found being around him easy. Physical contact always resulted in some form of sexualised, inappropriate behaviour. Personal hygiene was, and continues to be, a real issue for him.'

'What you're saying suggests a lot more than neglect.'

'Oh, most certainly.' He nodded vigorously. 'I couldn't agree with you more. But you see, we have nothing to go on other than the boy's physical condition on admission. His behaviour was, and remains, indicative of severe physical abuse at the very least, but I'm afraid that's as much as I can say about it.'

'How is he around his mother? What's their relationship like?'

'I'd have to say he is as close to her as he is to anyone here.'

'But you have indicated that he isn't close to either you or your team.'

'Exactly. He goes through the motions, but he has never given any indication that he has any feelings for her at all. There have been periods when she has disappeared for weeks at a time—gone off with boyfriends, we think. There has been no alteration to his behaviour, either for better or worse.'

'Did he request the access visits?' I asked.

'No. They were suggested by a child psychologist. Collette went along with it, and Edgar didn't seem to care, so they have continued, off and on, for the last three years.' Hugh paused. 'The problem is, he doesn't care about *anything*. He doesn't mind offending anyone. I've seen him being really chastised by a teacher, and he simply sits there placidly—no reaction. He will plan, over the long term, an act he knows will really hurt and upset someone, yet he'll show neither amusement nor remorse when he carries it out and causes the grief he so carefully plotted. He is—you'll just have to make up your own mind. I don't want to influence your feelings about him.'

There didn't seem much else to say. It was clear that Hugh, as Melanie had been, was very conflicted about this strange boy.

'I suppose I'd better go out and have a chat with him, then,' I said, standing up, and immediately realising that I'd moved too quickly: my head pounded in protest.

Hugh showed me into a sparsely decorated lounge. It had a bare wooden floor, with a ragged mat in the centre, and a variety of armchairs and beanbags about its periphery. A rather ancient-looking television sat forlornly in one corner. I waited. Finally, the manager returned with Edgar in tow.

'He was out looking at your car,' Hugh said. 'Jeepers, I haven't seen one of those Austin Allegros in years.'

'Yeah, you don't come across too many these days.'

'I think my uncle used to drive one, back in the day.'

I smiled, wishing he'd just go so I could start getting to know my new client. The child in question was standing, once again completely motionless, behind Hugh. He wasn't looking at me. His eyes were fixed on the television. Suddenly, in a burst of movement, he strode over to it and switched it on.

'Edgar, it's not time for telly now, please,' Hugh said. 'And, anyway, you're not in school today because you've been so naughty. So you're certainly not going to spend the time you should be in lessons watching children's programmes.'

He hit the off switch, and the screen went dead. Edgar barely seemed to register the act: he remained gazing at the screen.

'Now, I hope you're not going to be nasty to Shane,' Hugh continued, looking at the brooding boy.

'We'll be fine, Hugh,' I said. 'Why don't you leave us to it? I bet you've got plenty of work to do.'

'You sure?' Hugh asked, obviously far from certain about deserting me.

'Positive. I'll call you if I need you.'

Reluctantly, he turned on his heel. I sighed quietly and walked over to where Edgar was standing, still looking at the dead TV screen. I noticed the table it was on had wheels. Slowly, I pushed it aside. Edgar remained staring at the spot it had just vacated for a moment, then he turned sharply to me.

'Are you a queer?' he asked me. His voice was almost toneless. He spoke quite clearly and each word was enunciated perfectly, but the sentence was without inflection of any kind. There wasn't even the slightest rise at the end to denote a question.

'Why do you think I'm gay, Edgar?' I asked, fascinated.

'Hugh is a queer. He takes it up the arse from other men,' was the response.

'And how do you know that?'

As if I hadn't asked the question, Edgar turned and pulled over a beanbag. His movements were strange also. It was as though he couldn't move his neck properly. When he had to look at something, he turned his entire body in its direction.

Bending his knees to get on the correct level, he punched a depression in the bag, and then awkwardly settled himself into it.

'Comfortable?' I asked.

'You look like a fag,' Edgar said, trying a different tack.

I sat down in the nearest chair. 'You seem to be very interested in homosexuality,' I said. 'Do you think that maybe you're gay?'

'No.'

The barest hint of a smile played about the boy's lips. He's teasing me, I thought. Well, let's play along and see what happens.

'You've been expelled from school. What happened there?'

'Do you fancy Hugh?'

I sighed. 'I'll tell you what, Edgar. Let's make a deal. If you answer my questions honestly, I'll answer yours. How does that sound?'

He looked at me expressionlessly. 'Okay.'

'Right. So, why'd you get kicked out of school?'

'I set a fire in the classroom.'

'Why'd you do that?'

'I like fires.'

'Have you lit fires in school before?'

'Yeah. Now it's my turn. Are you a homo?'

'No.'

'Do you fancy Hugh?'

'If I'm not gay, I'm hardly going to fancy Hugh, am I?'

'Do you like looking at men's arses?'

'I've already answered that question,' I said. 'Are you glad you've been expelled, Edgar?'

'I don't care. I hate them all.'

'The teachers?'

'Everyone.'

'Is that why you lit the fire? Did you want to kill them?'

His smile grew broader. 'I *could* have killed them.'

'So why didn't you?'

'Me now. Do you like wearing women's clothes?'

I shook my head. 'Do I look that fashion conscious?'

'I bet you do when you're at home, when nobody can see you.'

'Is that the way you want to do this, Edgar? If you're not happy with my answers, you're just going to make things up?'

He made a noise that could have been a laugh, except that there was neither joy nor mirth in it. 'You like to ride boys, you do,' he said.

We sat there for a time, him virtually leering at me. Finally, I said, 'Do people call you gay, Edgar? Is that what this is about? Did they call you queer?'

The boy looked at me curiously, as if I were a strange insect that had crawled from beneath a stone unexpectedly. 'No,' he said, stood up, and left the room.

I stayed where I was for ten minutes, in case he came back, and then I went to find Hugh.

'Well, what do you make of him?' he said when I knocked on the door of his office.

I shrugged. 'He's challenging, there's no doubt about that.'

The manager fiddled with some papers on his desk awkwardly, motioning for me to sit down. 'What did you talk about?'

I thought for a moment. Deciding on the truth, I said, 'About how everyone's gay.'

'Ah.' Hugh stood up and walked to the window. 'He told you I'm gay, I suppose.'

'He also told me I was, so I didn't put much pass on it,' I said.

'I am gay, though, Shane.'

I wasn't surprised. 'So?'

'It's a bit of a cliché, isn't it? A homosexual man, working with children?'

I was feeling wretched by then. My head had settled into a rhythmic, droning thump, and dehydration was making me nauseous and irritable. 'Listen, Hugh,' I said, as patiently as I could, 'I know all types of people who work with children. My boss, Ben Tyrrell, was pioneering revolutionary approaches to child protection back in the seventies when men weren't even heard of in this line of work, and he's straight. It's still a female-dominated profession, but there are more and more guys coming into it all the time.' I could tell I wasn't convincing him, so I tried another tack. 'I haven't done any research on this, but I reckon the statistics on how many male childcare workers are gay probably reflects the same balance as in any other profession. So, while you're still a minority, you're far from the only gay in the village. I mean, one of my colleagues at the Trust is a lesbian, I think, although it's not something she talks about. And frankly, why the fuck should she? I'm heterosexual. It's not something I feel the need to advertise. To each his own.'

Hugh was watching me solemnly, obviously trying to gauge my response. He still wasn't sure where he stood with me. 'Yes, but if Edgar is going to make an issue out of it, don't you think I'm likely to run into difficulties?'

'No. Could I have a glass of water?'

'What? Are you all right? You look awful.'

'Yeah, I'd just like some water, that's all. Please.'

'Certainly, just a moment.'

While he was gone, I tried to gather my thoughts. This was not a conversation I had been prepared for, and I wasn't in a position to give particularly enlightened advice. I am not a person who can say 'some of my best friends are gay'. I have *some* gay friends, but the truth is, the majority of my close friends and associates are heterosexual, or are so in the closet I haven't noticed either way. I had a suspicion, however, that there was more to this than just a fear of stereotyping.

When Hugh returned, with a tall glass full of iced water, complete with a wedge of lemon, I tried to give voice to my real concerns.

'Hugh, I can't help but wonder why you're telling me all this. I mean, I've never met you before today. Shouldn't you be talking to one of your staff, or your supervisor, maybe?'

He sat opposite me and put his head in his hands for a long moment. I seemed to have hit a raw nerve. He didn't want to look at me. 'It's *because* I don't know you that it's easy to talk about it. You won't judge me.'

'Oh, come on. How do you know I'm not some rednecked homophobe? I mean, look at me. I easily could be.'

'I just knew you weren't. Your eyes—'

'Are bloodshot and half closed today.'

'No, you have kind eyes.'

I sipped some of the water. I could almost sense it spreading through me. I felt like a plant must when it's been watered. 'You haven't come out to your team, have you?'

He paused. 'No.'

'Or your boss.'

'No.'

'What about your family?'

'I think they know. It just ... hasn't come up in conversation.'

I nodded. Some children, particularly those who have been really badly abused, develop a talent for finding the right buttons to push. It's as if they have an in-built magnifying glass, and they use it to find all the minuscule chinks in their targets' armour. Hugh didn't wear make-up, nor did he have a Freddie Mercury T-shirt or walk about singing show tunes. He wasn't camp, by any means, yet there was a certain air about him that implied a degree of ambiguity.

'I bet Edgar harps on this pretty constantly.'

'I know he directed the same diatribe at you, but I'm the only male on the team here.'

'And he might just have used the same line on me as a way of telling me about you.'

'Yes. That's what I think, if I'm honest.'

I drank some more water. Life was beginning to ebb back into me. 'Well, he's told me, and I don't care. If your team haven't made a big deal about it, I'd just stop worrying. If you aren't ready to come out to them, don't. That's really as much advice as I can give you.'

'Ireland isn't half as enlightened as we'd all like to think,' Hugh said, slowly. 'In a lot of people's minds, homosexuality and paedophilia are strongly linked.'

'Is that what you're worried about?'

'I'd be a fool not to be.'

'How long have you been doing this kind of work?' I asked him.

'Almost twenty years.'

'And in all that time, have there been any allegations or claims of malpractice made against you?'

'No. Never.'

'And I presume you didn't just become gay within the past couple of years?'

He laughed. 'No. I've been a confirmed bachelor since adolescence. Maybe even before that.'

'Well then. I think you have a proven track record of being safe, don't you? This is none of my business, and please don't be offended, but do you have a partner?'

'Yes. David and I have been together for five years, now.'

'And David is, I presume, a consenting adult.'

'He's forty-six.'

'Then what the fuck do you have to worry about? You are an educated, professional man in a long-term relationship. You have an unblemished work record, and under the current equality legislation, nobody, regardless of any suspicions they might have, can question you about what you do or with whom you do it outside the workplace, so long as what you're doing doesn't break any laws. If you wanted to dress up as fucking Judy Garland and parade down O'Connell Street with a group of transsexual circus performers during rush hour, it's your own affair.'

'That sounds like fun, actually.' Hugh grinned. He sat back, looking sheepish. 'I'm sorry to have offloaded all that on you. You've kind of put it into some perspective for me.'

'Have I?' I laughed. 'I appreciate your saying so, because I have to tell you, I was not in my comfort zone.'

'I know. Thanks for trying. It's just that Edgar ... has a way of making me feel more than a little inadequate. It's that dead-eyed stare of his, I think. I have never met a child quite like him. Do you know, I've considered requesting a transfer, just to get away from him?'

'He seems to have that effect on people,' I said.

'I hope you're up to the challenge.'

It was my turn to look sheepish, as I pondered the fact that, this morning, at least, I wasn't really up to any challenges.

Chapter 6 ∽

When I got out to the gate, Edgar was standing there, waiting for me.

'When are you coming to see me again?' he asked.

'One day next week,' I told him, surprised at the renewed interest.

'And what are we going to do? If you want me to talk about stuff at home, or my mammy, you might as well not bother.'

'No. I was thinking we might just hang. Go out for a walk, maybe to the park ... whatever you want. It'll be your time to do with as you wish. Why don't you think about it between now and then?'

Edgar eyed me. It felt like I was being X-rayed.

'Okay,' he said, and walked past me towards the house. 'Oh,' he said, as he reached the front door, 'Hugh's right. He's a clever old puff, really. You do have a nice car.'

'Thanks,' I said, genuinely pleased by this statement. With me, flattery will get you everywhere. 'I'm glad you like it.'

'I've let the air out of all your tyres, by the way,' he said matter-of-factly, and went inside.

In my weakened state, it took a few moments for that information to sink in. I slowly turned, and saw that he had been telling the truth. Each of the four tyres of my car was completely flat. Muttering impotently, I went over and examined the damage.

It seemed that, despite my worst fears, Edgar had not slashed the tyres. He must have used a sharp tool to depress the air valve, deflating them that way. I sat on the ground, laid my head against the cool metal of my car door, and pulled out my mobile phone.

'Ger, I've run into a spot of grief,' I told my mechanic when he picked up. 'Do you have an air pump that'll travel?'

My erstwhile car doctor informed me that it would be mid-afternoon before he'd be available to come to my aid. I wasn't sure that I was comfortable leaving my precious automobile to Edgar's tender mercies for the five intervening hours, so I rang Mrs Munro and asked her to cancel my afternoon appointments, climbed in, locked the door behind me, and pushed the seat back.

As I closed my eyes, getting comfortable for the wait, I wondered about what my new friend had just done. The flats were irritating, certainly, and would cost me a few euro. But the prank wasn't really serious. It was, I thought, a shot across my bows. This, Edgar was telling me, is just a sample of what I'm capable of.

What would he try next?

Chapter 7 ～

I found out from Irma that Elvira usually dropped Litovoi off at the crèche at eleven in the morning which, I reasoned, meant her shift at the hotel started at midday.

So, at nine on Monday, I knocked on the door of the one-bedroomed flat the Tomescu family called home. Elvira answered, and the expression on her face when she saw me made up for any lack of fluency in English: she was unreservedly horrified.

'No,' she said, trying to close the door just as I inserted my boot. 'I already say I no see you. My son no see you. Go away from my home, please.'

Litovoi peered around his mother's legs, still dressed in a faded pair of Teletubby pyjamas. 'Shane! *Ce mai faci?*'

'*Mulțumesc, bine*,' I said, waving at the child. 'Can I come in, please, Elvira? I'm not here to give you a hard time. I'll only stay a few minutes.'

'If my husband finds out, he will be very angry,' the woman said, looking up and down the street, as if her enraged spouse would suddenly spring from a doorway and pounce on us. They lived just outside the city centre, in an area that had already been unofficially christened Po-Land by the few remaining Irish locals.

'Why do you think he'd be annoyed, Elvira? I'm not suggesting you've done anything wrong. In fact, I'd like to apologise to you about how I acted the other day when you came to see me.'

That stopped her in her tracks. 'You apologise to me?'

'Yes. I was insensitive.'

She shook her head, puzzled.

I realised the word was new to her, so I rephrased it: 'I was rude to you. I didn't understand what you were trying to tell me. I just want to talk to you for a little while, then I promise you that I'll go.'

Begrudgingly, she stepped aside, and allowed me access. The flat was small, dark and damp. The building itself had been altered very little from the days of the tenements, and the atmosphere seemed to have soaked up all the unhappiness of countless families who had ticked off the interminable days and nights they had wasted there.

Elvira had done her best to make the most of the place. Every surface was spotless, and the carpet, which was threadbare in many places, was covered here and there with mats that looked as though they had been hand-crocheted from those kits you can buy in craft shops. I was about to sit on the couch, when I noticed one leg was broken, and the entire seat lurched precariously to one side. I remained standing.

'What do you want?' Elvira asked, her voice weary, her face lined with care.

'To tell you that I want to help you—but to let you know that that means I am offering you the kind of help you need, not the kind of help I think you need.'

She shook her head. 'I do not understand.'

'I want *you* to tell me what you need.'

She laughed at that, and sat down on a wooden kitchen chair that stood in one corner. Litovoi was watching us wide-eyed, his thumb stuck into his mouth. I hadn't known he sucked his thumb. He certainly didn't while at the crèche.

'*A merge ina dormiter*, Craig,' Elvira said to the child, who scampered through one of the doors adjoining the room, and left us alone together.

As soon as the door closed, she turned her full, venomous gaze upon me.

'You want to know what help I need?' she spat.

'Yes. I do.'

'We need money. Lots of money.'

This was what I had been waiting for. It might not appear to be much, but it was a doorway, a crevice for me to get my fingers into.

'Okay,' I said. 'I might not be able to give you actual money, but I can still make life a little easier.'

'*Ack*.' The sound was guttural and filled with disgust. 'You go now, please. You talk, is all. No good for me.'

'No, listen.' I looked about the room, and my eyes fell on the damaged couch. 'Your sofa is broken.'

She looked at it. 'Sofa and bed. Yes. It broke. No use, now.'

'You use it to sleep on?'

She sighed. 'My husband sleep here. He sometimes finish work in the middle of the night, and he not want to wake up Craig and me, so he sleep here.'

'That can't be very comfortable. Not when it's all wobbly and leaning to one side.'

'I think he sleep on floor, now.'

I took a deep breath, and made my play. 'I could get you a new couch. A proper sofabed. One that folds out so you can tuck it away during the day.'

She looked at me. 'I no understand.'

'I can organise for you to have a new couch.'

She shook her head. 'How?'

'The people I work for have a fund for things like this. I'd have to get it approved, but I'm fairly sure that by the end of this week, we could have a brand new couch for you and your family.'

She laughed and waved the thought away. 'No. You make fun of me. We are not from Ireland. Nobody wishes to help us.'

I stood up and extended my hand. 'I give you my word,' I said. 'I promised you I wanted to do something for you. Now, let me show you that I'm serious.'

She took my hand gently, but stayed sitting down. 'That is nice,' she said, the fight gone out of her now. 'You come see me again when you have new couch for me. Then we will see.'

'I'll do that,' I said. 'You'll see me very soon.'

———

Accessing the money, as I suspected, wasn't a big issue. The Dunleavy Trust is funded from the estate of a ludicrously wealthy Irish-American; she had died in Boston and had bequeathed her fortune to help the troubled families of her birth city.

This did not mean handouts—the policy Ben had developed was rooted in helping people to help themselves. So, while the trust would often spend large amounts of money on furniture, decorating and, on occasion, had even purchased mobile homes for members of the travelling community, it stopped short of simply giving away wads of cash.

———

I met Elvira outside the hotel where she worked the following evening. I had rung ahead, so she was expecting me. The air had that pleasant pink glow it gets in spring, when the day is balancing on the cusp of night, and people on their way home from work were dawdling in an unhurried manner, as if dinner could wait.

Elvira crossed the road, dodging traffic. She was not really smiling, but obviously, for the first time, was not completely unhappy to see me.

'We buy a sofa?' she said, raising her eyebrows.

'Yep. Why don't we go and look at some? It's late opening in most of the larger shops.'

She stood for a moment, eyeing me uncertainly. 'How you get money for this?'

'I told you—the people I work for have lots of money. It was easy.'

'I cannot pay you back.' She was chewing ferociously on her lower lip. It had not even occurred to me that she might think that, and I felt like kicking myself.

'It's not a loan, Elvira. This is a gift. You don't have to pay me back.'

'You want something else?'

This was not how I had expected the conversation to go. 'No. Thank you, but you're grand. No repayments.'

Suddenly she smiled, and it transformed her face. 'No repayments?'

I smiled back, relieved the conversation was over. 'That's right. Is someone looking after Litovoi, or shall we go and pick him up?'

'He is with his father.'

'Okay,' I said. 'Does Petru know we're going furniture shopping?'

The young woman considered this question. 'I will tell him when we have nice sofa picked out.'

I shrugged. 'You know best.'

It didn't take long to find one. Elvira knew what she wanted, and, to my utmost surprise, before we had left the second store, the purchase was made. The couch would be delivered later that evening.

'So,' I said, as we stood on the street outside, 'I've given them a few quid to take the old couch away. You don't have room for it, and it's not worth getting mended.'

'Thank you,' Elvira said. 'The new one is very nice. Very good for my husband to sleep on.'

We stood there, an uncomfortable silence between us. 'Do you want to get something to eat before you go home?' I asked, for want of anything else to say.

'No, thank you. Petru will be waiting for me.'

'Okay, then. Can I call in and see you next week, perhaps? Check in on Litovoi?'

She looked exasperated. 'Why you no call him Craig?'

I grinned at her. 'We've already had this conversation. But I'll tell you what. Litovoi, you and me can sit down and have a chat about it, maybe? What do you say?'

'You can come in the morning,' she said, 'before I go to work.'

I nodded. 'I will.'

She began to walk away, picking up speed as if she needed to escape me as fast as she could. 'Enjoy the couch,' I said quietly to myself, and watched her as she disappeared into the crowd.

Chapter 8 ∾

I was heading out for lunch the next day when my mobile phone rang.

'Shane, it's Irma, over at Little Treasures nursery.'

'Yeah, hi, Irma,' I said. 'What can I do for you?'

'You'd better get over here.'

'What's the problem?'

'It's Craig.'

'Litovoi?'

'Yeah, whatever.' I suddenly realised she sounded scared to death.

'What's wrong with him?'

'I ... I think he's injured.'

'Have you called a doctor?'

'Yes, but ... well, I don't believe this was an accident.'

'What?'

'It looks like his arm is broken, and he's covered in bruises.'

'I'll be there as soon as I can.'

——

When I arrived, she brought me to the office where the boy was curled up on a seat, his cheeks wet with tears and pain etched across every millimetre of his face. I knelt down beside him.

'Hey, Litovoi. *Cum te simți?*'—'How are you?'

He looked at me, his eyes deep with pain.

'*Eu am durerea,*' he said quietly.—'I hurt.'

I didn't touch him. I am not a doctor, but I didn't need to look closely to see that something was terribly wrong. He was holding his arm at an odd angle, trying to support it across his knees. His breath seemed to be catching every now and again, and I guessed that his ribs were either severely bruised or possibly even broken. His face, I noticed, was untouched. I thought it unlikely he had somehow fallen, or maybe been knocked down by a car, without sustaining so much as a scratch to his face.

'*Ce s-a întâmplat*, Litovoi?' I asked.—'What happened?'

The boy looked at me for a moment, and I thought he was actually going to answer my question, but then his lower lip began to tremble, his face collapsed just like a building toppling, and he began to cry bitterly. I glanced up at Irma for some kind of support, but she looked as if she was about to start crying, too.

'*El este* okay,' I said.—'It's okay.' '*Nu ţi face griji.*'—'Don't worry.'

These were completely ridiculous things to say under the circumstances, but my mind had gone blank.

I heard voices at the office door; it opened and a middle-aged man in a suit, carrying a leather satchel, came in—obviously the doctor. I stepped back, and allowed him to do his job. The man, who introduced himself as Dr James Morrissey, gently picked up the patient and carried him to the room where the younger children took naps, and laid him on one of the low beds. I stood at the door while he carried out his examination. When he pulled up the child's T-shirt, I could see that Litovoi was indeed a patchwork of bruises and abrasions. There was an area on the left side of his chest that was a particularly disturbing shade of mottled blue.

Throughout the entire process, Litovoi cried quietly, every now and again muttering something in Romanian, scraps of words and phrases I couldn't understand. I felt nervy and agitated. I wanted to go over and hold the boy, but I knew enough to realise that I would do more harm than good if I did. Children who have just been abused can often become confused about what has happened to them. Close physical contact could make Litovoi feel as if he was being hurt again, or cause him to project his fears on to me. So I stayed back, and simply watched as the doctor, gently and with great skill and sensitivity, examined him.

Finally, without turning, he fumbled in his bag and produced a bottle and a syringe. 'I'm giving him a strong painkiller,' he said as he administered the injection. 'It'll make him sleep for a while but, things being as they are, that's desirable.'

'How bad is he?' I asked.

'He needs to be hospitalised, and an X-ray will tell us precisely what we're dealing with, but in my humble opinion, his arm is broken in two places, he has one, maybe two broken ribs, and I'm concerned there may be internal injuries, possibly to his spleen. Somebody gave this poor boy a very severe beating.'

'Could it have been an accident? Hit and run?'

Dr Morrissey gave a dry chuckle. 'Come over here for a moment.'

I did.

'Take a look at this.'

Litovoi was already drifting off, the drugs taking him in their grip. The doctor gently extended the child's unbroken arm. There, in stark relief against the paleness of his skin, was a dark bruise, clearly in the shape of an adult hand. Someone had grasped him with such force, they had left a mark.

'Cars don't usually leave bruises like that,' Dr Morrissey said.

'No,' I said, feeling anger building up inside me, 'they don't.'

Litovoi stirred, still muttering snatches of something. I reached over and stroked his hair, as the flashing lights of an ambulance appeared through the opaque glass of the window.

An hour later I was sitting in a waiting area in the City Hospital, drinking foul vending-machine coffee from a styrofoam cup. Elvira came in through the sliding doors, looking pale and frightened, accompanied by a tall, slim, sallow-skinned man dressed in scuffed jeans, work boots and a black leather jacket over a grey hoodie. I guessed this was Petru.

'Where is my son?' Elvira blurted out.

'He's down at X-ray,' I said. 'Irma, from the crèche, is with him.'

She nodded and rushed over to the counter, jabbering something to her husband as she went. He remained standing in front of me, apparently ignoring her.

'You are the furniture man,' he said.

I set the coffee aside on a low plastic table that divided the uncomfortable plastic chairs. 'And you must be Petru,' I said.

'I will give you some friendly advice,' he said. 'You should keep your nose out of my family's business.' He spoke with an accent, but obviously had much better English than his wife.

'I haven't been bothering your family,' I said. 'Part of my job is to assist with pre-school childcare which is how I met Litovoi. Elvira came to visit me, and then I offered to help you get a new couch because you needed one. Hardly what you'd call harassment, is it?'

He idly glanced over at where Elvira was still speaking to the girl on reception.

'What kind of a man makes his living working with children? That is no job for a man. Where I come from, that is woman's work.'

I grinned up at him. I was used to this type of comment, and it had long since stopped bothering me. 'Well, Petru, you've made your home where *I* come from, and here, things are a little bit different.'

The man snorted, and sat down beside me. I could smell sweat, engine oil and tobacco. 'No. Things are not so different,' he said. 'How you say? Same shit, different day?'

'Yes. They do say that,' I agreed.

'Well, for me, it is same shit, different place. Nothing has changed for us.' He sat with one leg slung over the other. He seemed relaxed and at ease, but I got the sense he was taking in everything that was going on around him.

'Do you have any thoughts about how your boy ended up beaten to within an inch of his life?' I asked.

Petru sucked air in through his teeth, making a whistling sound. 'No. I do not know what happened to him. I was at work last night, and I came home and went to sleep. I did not see him.'

'And nobody else was around the house? You didn't have any friends staying over?'

'No. No friends. We are too busy to have friends come to visit us. They all work, too.'

'You know the police will want to talk to you,' I said to him. I thought that fact might get a reaction.

'Yes, yes. I know. The police always like to have conversations with me. I am used to it.'

Elvira came back over to us. She said something so quickly in Romanian it sounded like a blur of noise to me.

'No, you go,' Petru said, in English. 'I will stay and speak to Harvey Norman here. We have not had a chance to get to know one another.'

Elvira made no comment, but walked very quickly and stiffly up the corridor towards the X-ray department.

'Petru,' I said, when she had gone, 'Litovoi is badly hurt. The doctor believes he may have internal injuries. There is the mark of a hand on his arm—that means that somebody purposely hurt him.'

Petru nodded. 'Yes. It must mean that,' he said.

'Aren't you angry? Upset?' I asked.

'Yes,' Petru said, turning to me, his face passive and his voice neutral. 'I am very angry. I am angry all the time. I am cross because my family came a long way to get to a country where we were told we could live a good life. Then we get here and it is just as bad as at home. I am pissed off because I hardly ever see my wife—she is asleep when I come home and at work when I get up. I am upset because people like you come sniffing about my home and my family. I have many reasons to be mad, furniture man. Craig being hurt is just another thing to add to a long list.'

'That's plenty to be pissed off about,' I agreed.

'I am not a patient man,' Petru continued. 'I am used to simple rules. If someone annoys me, I hurt them. If someone bothers my family, I bother theirs. Do you understand?'

I stiffened slightly. 'I think I do,' I said. 'But I've got to tell you, Petru, things aren't simple. Where children are concerned, matters can get very complicated indeed.'

Petru considered this, whistling tunelessly. 'I don't think so,' he said. 'I think you might be wrong there.'

I watched him. I had seen his type many times before. I was not afraid of him, but I was not stupid either. Petru Tomescu had an organisation behind him that was capable of untold violence, and had very few scruples about who they directed it at. I chose my words carefully.

'I'm going to be straight with you, Petru,' I said. 'I don't care what you're involved in. I don't care how you came here, or if you're legal. I don't care if Petru is your real name. My only concern is the welfare and safety of your little boy. Now, I don't doubt that you have a whole army of guys behind you who could make my life pretty miserable if they wanted to. But see, so have I. I have the police and the social services and one or two other agencies you probably haven't heard of besides.'

His face registered no response to this. We might have been

having a pleasant chat.

'I could have those people all over you,' I continued. 'But, see, I don't want to do that. I'd prefer to help you, to try and make your life better, if I can.'

'I do not need your help,' he said, deadpan.

'Maybe,' I said, realising I was never going to win with this man, 'maybe you don't. But I want you to understand something.'

'What is that, furniture man?'

'If I find out that you did this to Litovoi, I *will* make things difficult for you. And I don't care who your friends are, or how unpleasant they can be. Are we clear?'

'I understand,' he said.

We sat in silence for a while. He remained completely motionless. If his eyes hadn't been open, I would have thought he was asleep.

'I am going for a smoke,' he said after several minutes of nothing, and without ceremony stood up and walked towards the door.

'I'm all right,' I said to his back. 'I'll just wait here.'

He went outside, and the automatic doors slid closed behind him. I picked up a magazine from a collection in a rack by the window. There was a story in it about a woman from Fulham who had discovered that her husband was, in fact, married to four other women and had homes and children with all of them. I admired his energy, but thought that he probably needed to get a hobby.

'Shane.'

I looked up. Elvira was standing in front of me.

'How is he?' I asked.

'He hurt bad,' she said. 'They keep him here.'

I nodded. This was not news to me.

The woman was bobbing and swaying in an alarming manner. I noticed that, even though her face had a deathly pallor, there were deep red blotches on both cheeks.

'Sit down, Elvira,' I said, 'before you fall down.'

She did, virtually collapsing into the seat.

'Are you all right?' I asked her.

'My son ...' she said, but before she could say anything else, she broke down. I put my arm round her shoulder, and let her cry.

Hospitals are places where grief is not uncommon, and we sat, cocooned in our private pain, while the crowds, oblivious, milled about us, creating a white noise of chatter and motion. I held her, patting her shoulder occasionally, unsure what else to do. We were barely at the point where we were even on speaking terms, and I didn't know if I was really giving her any comfort at all. Finally she raised her head and pushed away from me. I squeezed her shoulder gently before removing my arm, and noticed that she winced and cringed at my touch. I sat up, and very delicately turned her to face me.

'You are hurt too?' I asked her.—'*Dus suntepi rānit de asemenea?*'

She tried to turn away from me, but I continued to hold her shoulders as gently as I could.

'How did this happen?' I asked her. 'Who did this to you and Litovoi?'

She just stared at me blankly, that feverish colour in her cheeks seeming to become even more florid. Sweat beaded her brow and formed a film over her upper lip. Without warning, her eyes rolled upwards in her head and she sagged in my arms.

'Shit,' I muttered, and hollered for a nurse.

As Elvira was placed on a trolley and wheeled towards casualty, I realised Petru had not returned from his cigarette. I excused myself, and ran out to the outdoor smoking area. Other than a heavily pregnant teenager in a knobbly pink dressing gown and elephant slippers, it was empty. Petru had gone.

Chapter 10

Elvira didn't regain consciousness for three hours. An examination showed that she, too, had been severely beaten, but other than cuts, bruises and sprains she had not been badly injured.

'She's in shock,' a young Asian doctor told me. 'She'll be fine.'

I thought that was a slightly simplistic view, but I kept my opinion to myself. Having had my fill of the out-of-date magazines, I bought a copy of *David Copperfield* from a small collection of cut-price paperbacks in the hospital shop, and was becoming reacquainted with Salem House and the redoubtable Steerforth when Elvira stirred and then shot bolt upright in bed. She had been placed in a public ward, but the nurses had pulled a curtain about her, so we had some privacy.

'Hey,' I said, going over and shushing her gently. 'You're okay. Just relax.'

Her eyes remained wide for a moment, but then she seemed to process the information and realised where she was. She settled back on to the pillows. I poured some water into a glass and handed it to her. She drank deeply.

'Litovoi,' she said, when the glass was empty. I thought it was interesting that she reverted to his birth name in this time of crisis.

'He's still asleep,' I said, pouring more water for her. 'The doctors have fixed up his arm, and they seem happy that he isn't hurt internally.' I searched for the Romanian word. 'Interior ... um ... *organe interne?*'

She nodded and closed her eyes. 'He will be all right?'

'I think so. But this has been very upsetting for him. And for you.'

Tears trickled from the corners of her eyes and dribbled on to the white pillow case.

'Where is my husband?'

'I don't know. He's gone,' I said. 'Elvira, did he do this to you?'

She turned to face the curtain.

'If you don't tell me, I can't help you. Has he been hurting you, Elvira? You and Litovoi?'

'It was not him. It was not Petru,' she said.

'Who, then?' I asked, but there was no reply.

I sat with her for an hour more, but she remained with her back to me. I didn't attempt to break the silence. I wanted her to see that my support was not conditional on her doing anything. I was there because I wanted to be.

As evening fell, I stood up.

'I'm going to go now, Elvira,' I said. 'I'll drop in on you tomorrow for a bit.'

I was just turning to push my way through the curtains, when she spoke. 'Shane.'

I paused. 'Yes?'

'Find my husband.'

I took a deep breath. This was a request I had not expected.

'The police are looking for him,' I said, truthfully.

'They will not find him.'

'Why not?'

She still lay facing the curtain, her back stiff in the blue hospital gown.

'Because he does not want them to. He is in much danger, Shane. You say you want help me and Litovoi. This is help. Find Petru.'

'Do you promise that it was not him who hit you?' I asked.

'I promise,' she said, her voice little more than a whisper.

'But you can't tell me who *did* hit you.'

A sob. 'I did not know them.'

'Them?'

'Yes. Two men.'

'Did they break in?' I asked.

'No. I let them in the front door,' she said.

'Why?'

'You no understand,' she said.

'Help me to understand, then.'

'I thought they come for money.'

I could hear the tea trolley as it began to make its rounds. There was the ambient sound of conversation, televisions, beeping medical machinery and telephones ringing. Inside the curtains, it was as if we were in a different zone of reality.

'And did they want money?' I asked her.

'I do not know. They hit me, knock me down, and then they take Litovoi, and they make me watch while they hit him. One hold me while the other hurt my boy.'

'And they didn't say anything?'

'No.'

I shook my head. Could this be true? I knew so little about the Romanian community that I felt I wasn't really in a position to judge the veracity of the story.

'Why didn't you call somebody when they left?' I said, trying to keep the anger from my voice. 'You sent Litovoi to the crèche with a broken arm, Elvira!'

'I did not know his arm broke. He no cry. He say he well. I ... I afraid we be sent back to Romania if police come. We cannot go home.'

I walked back over, and patted her on the arm. She didn't move.

'I'll see what I can do. I'm not promising anything, okay? But I'll try.' I patted her arm again, and then went through the curtains, rejoining the bright, bustling world of the hospital, and leaving Elvira to her thoughts.

Chapter 11 ∾

I was to see Edgar O'Sullivan the following afternoon for our first proper visit since he had deflated my tyres. I had arranged to meet Melanie Moorehouse in a pub near Bluecloud for lunch before I saw him, to fill her in on my previous experience with her unruly client, and to get any final words of advice or encouragement she had to offer.

For once, Melanie was already there when I arrived. She was sitting at a corner table of the busy bar, speaking very loudly into her mobile. Despite the fact that there was a fair buzz of conversation, clinking glasses and a TV switched on to the horse racing, I could still hear every word she said. Luckily, this was a social call.

'Yeah, Joanna, I'll see you there this evening. Is Marcus going to join us? ... Brilliant. I haven't seen that fucker in months ... Now, that's not nice. I know he's a bollix, but that's not his fault. I think it's genetic.' She paused, laughing riotously at her own joke. 'Okay. I'll be there around nine. Have a *large* Bacardi waiting for me, right? ... Yeah, see you later. Bye for a while.'

I slid into the seat opposite her.

'Hey, Shaneyo. How's it hangin'?'

I noticed she had a half-empty pint of lager in front of her. 'You finished for the day?' I said.

'Nah. Meetings all afternoon. Case conferences and shit. You know how it is.'

'Mmm. So, I have encountered our young Mr O'Sullivan ...'

I ordered an open smoked-salmon sandwich, and told her about my adventure at Bluecloud, leaving out Hugh's concerns about his sexuality. She sipped her beer and listened, guffawing heartily when I got to the state of my tyres.

'Oh, that is classic Edgar. Just classic.'

'It seems that I should develop eyes in the back of my head when I'm around him, that's for sure.'

'Where you planning on going this afto?'

'Nothing fancy or over-stimulating for a first session,' I said. 'I thought we'd maybe go and have something to eat, a chat, lay down some ground rules, and take it from there. Probably won't be more than an hour or so, today. I don't want to push things, y'know?'

'Absolutely. Don't expect much, okay? He's not what you'd call an open child. He may not even speak to you at all. I've spent entire visits with him when he didn't make a sound.'

'He spoke to me plenty the other day. It wasn't exactly what I'd call constructive, but he talked. I was sort of hoping that by being in a public place, he might be less inclined to behave offensively.'

Melanie took a swig of her beer. 'Don't count on it. I don't think he cares too much where he is.'

'I dunno. We're all socialised into not wanting to embarrass ourselves in front of a crowd of people. That's difficult to set aside.'

'I have to tell you that in my experience Edgar does not follow any of the accepted norms. He seems, in fact, to wilfully cast them aside.'

I had a bite of my sandwich. It was very good. 'I want you to think, Mel. Isn't there a single incident, during all the time you've spent with Edgar, that you saw a positive response to something you did with him? I mean, even a reaction that was less negative than usual?'

She lit a cigarette and sat back, considering. 'I think he likes books,' she said at last.

'That's something,' I said. 'Tell me about it. How do you come to that conclusion?'

'I've noticed that he has a load of books in his room. And he seems to enjoy going to the library and to bookshops.'

'That it?'

'I know it's not much, but it's all I've got.'

I shrugged. 'It's something. I'll have to see what I can do with it.'

She drained what was left in her glass and stood up. 'I'm getting another one. Can I get you anything?'

'I'm good,' I said.

'Suit yourself.'

'There's one other thing,' Melanie said, when she returned with her pint.

'Yeah?'

'We were going past the old grain stores the other day.' She was referring to an area of old warehouses that had once been part of a brewery that had not operated since the turn of the twentieth century. They had mostly been converted into flats. 'He asked me a lot of questions about them. I didn't really have any information, and that seemed to annoy him. Maybe he's a closet historian.'

'Perhaps,' I said. 'Mel, I think you've just given me an idea.'

'I aim to please,' she said, raised her glass and gulped down one third of it.

Chapter 12

E dgar and I stood outside St Peter's Church in Drogheda later that afternoon.

'Are we going to Mass?' he asked, looking up at the huge, grey building.

'No. There's something inside I thought you might be interested in,' I said.

'What? God?'

'No. It's something kind of cool, and kind of gross, too. Maybe you wouldn't be able for it. Let's just go and have a cup of tea, eh?'

I began to walk down the steep steps that led back to the pavement. This was a gamble. I didn't know if he'd follow, go on inside without me, or simply run off. I clenched my teeth, and resolved not to look back.

'Shane.'

I stopped. 'Yes, Edgar?'

'Let's go in, then. I want to see it.'

I turned, grinning. 'Good. I think you'll be impressed.'

———

Oliver Plunkett was born in Loughcrew, County Meath, in 1625. Oliver's youth was spent amid the upheaval of the rebellion against Charles I. His family, as members of the gentry class, publicly supported the king, while secretly conspiring to win freedom for the Irish. A literate and pious child, Oliver was sent at sixteen to Rome, to be instructed under Friar Pierfrancesco

Scarampi, a highly respected theologian. After completing his studies, Oliver was ordained and, due to the ongoing troubles in Ireland, was appointed to and maintained the chair of theology at the College de Propaganda Fide for twelve years. When Edmund O'Reilly, the archbishop of Armagh, died in 1669, Oliver took his place. He travelled to England, spending time hidden in the company of the almoner (the cleric responsible for the distribution of charitable donations) of Charles II. From there he travelled to Dublin in 1670.

Having arrived in his homeland, Oliver wasted no time. Within three months, he had convened a synod, performed two ordinations, and administered the sacrament of confirmation to 10,000 people. A determined and tenacious man, he engaged in numerous religious and political battles: lack of devotion among both clergy and laity was an issue that exercised his energies constantly, as did conflicts between the monastic orders, clergy and friars. He attempted to install the Jesuits to teach children and seminarians, and took a firm stance against the oppression of Roman Catholics by the Protestant civil authorities.

King Charles II began another round of religious persecution in 1673, and most bishops were forced to flee or go into hiding, with Oliver in the latter category. After an attempt on the king's life in 1678, believed to be linked to the Roman Church, all bishops and clerics were expelled from Ireland.

Mythology suggests that an excommunicated priest sold Oliver out while he was living under an assumed identity in London. At any rate, he was arrested and imprisoned in Dublin. The Crown alleged that Oliver was attempting to bring 40,000 French soldiers to England to secure a Catholic assassination plot. The prosecution were completely unsuccessful in substantiating their claims, however, and Oliver was transferred to London. There, in a kangaroo court, he was dubiously convicted of his crimes.

On the first of July 1681, Oliver Plunkett stood on the gallows at Tyburn. It is recorded that he showed remarkable calm and courage and prayed for the repose of his own soul, and publicly forgave his enemies. He was hanged, disembowelled and quartered. The various parts of his body were placed in tin boxes and buried in London. But they didn't stay buried in that city, and the story doesn't end there.

————

'So this is his head,' Edgar said, peering through the glass dome at the brown, skeletal, hairless face, its skin, thin as paper, stretched over the bones.

'Yes.'

'It's ugly.'

'It's more than three hundred years old,' I said. 'Most people's heads rot away after they're dead. It's remarkable there's anything left of it at all.'

'Why didn't his head rot, then?'

'When I was in school, they told me it was because he was a saint and that God didn't want his body to decompose.'

'And do you believe that?'

'Um ... well, if you look at that card there'—I indicated an information card that was hanging on the wall beside the relic— 'it says that a family of bugs moved into the head back in 1978, and they had to take it to a museum and treat it with special chemicals to stop it from falling apart. I'm not sure that would have happened if God had had anything to do with it.'

I know what you're thinking: what possessed me to bring an obviously emotionally disturbed child to see the mummified head of a man who had been tortured to death? It's a fair question.

Firstly, I wanted to find something he was interested in. Melanie had told me he had voluntarily asked a question about the grain stores, and that this was unusual for Edgar, demonstrating that he must have been very interested indeed. Oliver Plunkett was an Irish saint, and although he was born miles away from the city, I thought a little national history might help to give Edgar a sense of place. I felt that he didn't really belong anywhere. Knowing the background of your home makes it easier to contextualise it—it grounds you. Secondly, I hoped it would give us something to talk about that was neutral and unthreatening for him. I had no intention of getting into anything heavy or emotive on our first real session together. If nothing else, poor old Oliver would be a talking point. Finally, I was working on the premise that, despite the fact that he was so strange and empty, Edgar was an eleven-year-old boy, and boys like creepy disgusting things. You can't really get any creepier than a three-hundred-year-old head.

Edgar walked round to the other side of the case, to look at the macabre object from another angle. He moved slowly, his face close to the glass.

'He looks sad,' he said.

'If you think about what they did to him, that's not really surprising.'

'Why, what did they do?'

'He was hurt pretty badly before he was killed.'

'How?'

'You know how they used to hang people?' I said.

'Yeah.'

'And they also used to cut people's heads off?'

'Yeah.'

'They did both of those things, and cut him up as well.'

Edgar continued to look at the head, his face expressionless. 'Wouldn't just one of those things kill you?'

'It would. I suppose they wanted to be sure,' I said.

'And this was all because he was a priest?'

'He was an archbishop, which means he was, like, a fairly big guy in the Church. Kind of a captain of the priests. But it wasn't just that—they said he was trying to kill the king of England.'

'Was he?'

'No, I don't think so.'

'Why didn't they like priests?'

I scratched my own head, which was, thankfully, still attached to the rest of me. I hadn't expected him to be so interested. It seemed that Melanie had been right about his liking history. 'England was in charge of Ireland back then, and most people in England were Protestant, which is another religion, although it has similarities to Roman Catholicism, which is what most of us in Ireland are. Seeing as how the priests are the ones who tell us how to pray, and say Mass and look after the churches, I suppose the English thought that getting rid of them would be a way of stopping people being a part of that religion.'

'It didn't work, though, did it?'

'No. Look at how big this place is. People don't go to Mass so much any more, but the Church is still going.'

Edgar nodded, still completely focussed on the disembodied head in its glass case. I stood back, watching him.

'Why is he here?' he asked after a time.

'That's a good question. In the beginning, I reckon he was brought here because he's an Irish saint, and people wanted to have a part of him here to pray to. I've seen it in other countries, where they have fingers and toes and pieces of hair of local saints. It's kind of strange, I suppose, but years ago it gave people comfort. Now, I think, they keep him here because he's become part of this church. People come here to see him. I reckon if you were to ask one of the priests, they'd say Oliver was being honoured.'

Edgar turned and looked at me. His expression was, as usual, flat and devoid of emotion, but when he spoke, his voice betrayed something I had not heard from him before: sadness. 'I think he's lonely,' he said. 'A bit like an animal in the zoo. All these people come to gawk, but no one really cares about him. Why don't they just bury him and leave him in peace?'

'The head isn't him, Edgar,' I said, worried that this might not have been such a good idea. 'He's long gone. That's just an old piece of bone and dried-out skin. It doesn't feel anything.'

The boy looked at it again, and then met my eyes.

'He doesn't feel anything,' Edgar said, quietly. 'Just like me.'

Chapter 13 ∾

I brought a tray laden with cream cakes, a cup of coffee for me and a milkshake for Edgar to our table. The café was in the centre of a busy shopping mall near the church, and was one of those open-plan affairs: it was separated from the shopping centre's main thoroughfare by a low wall, so we could have reached out and touched the passing shoppers if we had wanted to.

Edgar pulled the strawberry milkshake over and dove in straight away. I thought about reminding him that 'thank you' was a small courtesy, but decided it wasn't worth the battle that was liable to ensue. I would leave that for another day.

I pushed the cakes into the centre of the table, and had some coffee. It was weak and lukewarm. But it was better than no coffee—just.

I lit a cigarette. 'So, any sign of you going back to school yet?'

The boy shook his head, still sucking up the sweet mixture through his straw.

'You're going to give yourself an ice-cream headache,' I warned him.

He shook his head again. I shrugged and lapsed into silence. This was his time, and we had talked quite a bit in the church. If he wanted some quiet, that was okay by me. Seconds later, I heard wet, slurping noises that told me he had finished the shake. He sat back, steadied himself, and belched cacophonously. I raised an eyebrow. 'No headache?'

'I don't get them,' he said, and picked up a cream doughnut, biting off half of it in one munch.

'Everyone gets ice-cream headaches, Edgar,' I said.

'Not me,' he said, cream and jam smeared about his mouth.

'Fair enough. Listen, I'd like to just clear up a few things about this time we're going to be spending together.'

He picked up a second cake. He was eating in a serious, systematic manner, as if it was his job to clear the plate. He didn't seem to be getting any pleasure from it, nor was he repelled by the food. It was just there, and he was going to consume it.

'My visits are really your time, Ed. Most often it'll just be you and me. I've asked Melanie if I can supervise some of the access visits between you and your mother, too, and she's quite happy for me to do that. So every now and again we'll have your mum along too. Is that okay?'

He nodded, chewing stolidly.

'Now,' I continued, 'I know that in the past you've been leaving Bluecloud for these types of sessions. We don't have to. If you want to hang out there, that's perfectly okay. If you want to go out, that's up to you, too. I'm very happy to come up with ideas for activities and things we can do, like I did today, but I think it'd be great if you could think of some, too. You can suggest anything you like; if it's within reason, I'll try and accommodate you.'

There was one cake left on the plate. He had now eaten three. I wondered if he'd ask me if I wanted it. He didn't.

'I want these visits to be as much fun as they can be,' I said. It felt very much as though I was talking to myself. Edgar was giving no sign that he heard or understood, was happy, sad or pissed off about what I was saying. I continued, doggedly, 'But there are just two rules that I do insist on. You always try your best, no matter what we do, and you don't hurt anyone, including yourself. Okay?'

A barely perceptible nod. The last cake was gone. I was amazed that he was not feeling sick. It suddenly occurred to me that perhaps that had been his plan all along: to gorge himself on ice cream and cake, only to spew it all over me like Regan in *The*

Exorcist. I decided it might be better not even to think about that.

'Is there anything you'd like to do next time?'

He sat across from me, staring at the empty plate. 'Can I have more cake?' he asked.

'I don't think so,' I said. 'Four is kind of a lot for one kid.'

'But I want more. You said you'd do what I want.'

'I also said I didn't want you to hurt yourself, and eating more cakes will make you sick, and give you one very large stomach ache, thereby hurting you.'

One of the things I love about those two rules (which I stole from Ben Tyrrell, actually) is that they can be applied to almost any situation with virtually every age group.

Edgar began to wipe the powdered sugar and crumbs off the empty plate with his finger. 'I'm still hungry. I got no lunch,' he said.

'You got no lunch?' I said, not even trying to keep the incredulity out of my voice. 'I find that very hard to believe.'

'I didn't—Bridget is on shift today, and she hates me.'

She's not alone in that sentiment, I thought, remembering my conversations with Melanie and Hugh, but kept the opinion to myself.

'She hates you so much she doesn't feed you?' I said, instead.

The plate licked clean, Edgar folded his arms, managing to simulate putting on a sulk while leaving his face completely passive. 'Yeah, that's right. She's a big fat mean bitch.'

'Maybe if you didn't speak to her like that, she'd warm to you a bit,' I suggested.

'I don't call her a bitch to her face,' he said.

'I bet you do.'

He said nothing to that—it was an argument he was clever enough to know he could never win. I stubbed out my cigarette and looked at him. 'So how come you didn't get lunch?'

He stared back at me silently.

'I'll tell you what, Edgar,' I said. 'You tell me the story of why you didn't get anything to eat for lunch—and don't give me any crap, mind; I want a believable tale, right? And if I think you're telling me the truth, I'll get you a sandwich. No more cakes, no more sweets or ice cream—a proper sandwich. Deal?'

Edgar continued to stare at me for a few moments, trying to work out if I was bluffing him. When he had satisfied himself that I was being genuine, he began to speak: 'Bridget and Hugh made lunch for themselves when I was out in the garden. I came in, and they were sitting there eating, and they hadn't made any for me. I got mad with them, and they sent me to my room.'

'So you got no food as a punishment?' I said. 'I don't believe that, Ed. That's not even a good try.'

'Hugh came up to me after a while and said I could come and have lunch, but that I'd have to make it myself,' the boy said. 'I didn't want to do that. I wanted them to say they were sorry and make it for me.'

I almost laughed. 'So you had no lunch because you were too stuck up to make your own?' I said. 'I'm afraid I don't have much sympathy for you.'

'That's their job,' Edgar said, as if he thought it was the most obvious thing in the world. 'They're supposed to look after me.'

'They are,' I said. 'But part of that is making sure you can do simple things, like make yourself a cheese sandwich. You're old enough to do stuff like that.'

Edgar didn't seem convinced. He began to stack the used knives, cup and plates, putting them to one side, making space for his next course. 'Can I have my food now, please?' he asked.

'Just one more thing first,' I said. 'When you were stomping off to your room, and telling Hugh and Bridget that you wanted them to make your lunch, did you call them names and say mean things to them?'

'That's my business,' Edgar said, his tone just as it had been, but the rhythm of the words suggesting annoyance.

I sighed. 'Do you want a sandwich or not?'

'Yes.'

'Well, then, I want to talk about this.'

He stopped clearing the cutlery. 'I called Hugh a big gay homo, and I called Bridget a fat smelly hooker.'

He said it so matter-of-factly, I had to bite my lip so as not to burst out laughing. When I was sure I could speak without creasing up, I said, 'Edgar, do you think that speaking to Hugh and Bridget like that is going to make them want to do anything for you?'

'They *have* to do things for me,' Edgar said. 'They're paid to. My mam told me.'

'They are,' I said. 'But wouldn't it be nice if they *wanted* to do things for you? When you do nice things for other people, they often do nice things in return. If you keep giving people grief—calling them names, playing mean tricks on them and stuff—that makes it hard for them to like you and do nice things for you.'

'But they have to anyway,' Edgar persisted. 'Right? They'd be fired if they don't.'

I shook my head. 'They'd be fired if they starved you, or hit you, or called you nasty names,' I said, 'but they won't be fired because they left you to make a snack for yourself when they could have done it for you. You see, that's the sort of thing people do for one another as an act of kindness. If you're not prepared to be kind, you can't really expect anyone to be especially kind to you.'

'I'll tell on them,' Edgar said. 'They'll have to do what I want.'

I could see that I was getting nowhere, so I gave up. 'What kind of sandwich do you want?' I asked.

'Can I have chips?' he said.

'No. A sandwich was the deal.'

'Chicken salad, then,' he said, 'and another milkshake.'

'Water or juice,' I said.

'Orange juice,' he said, and I thought I heard resignation in his voice.

I went up to the counter and gave the girl the order. She was constructing the sandwich when Edgar called me.

'Shane!'

I turned. He was standing up at our table, and had shouted my name quite loudly. Most of the people in the crowded café had turned to look.

'Yes, Ed?' I said.

'Shane, my mum used to give me blow jobs,' he said, enunciating each word slowly and carefully. 'She used to suck my dick, and then I'd go down on her and lick her out.'

Every other conversation in the restaurant stopped. It seemed that the shoppers wandering past all paused in their progress for a moment. I wished the ground would open up and swallow me. Edgar remained standing, waiting for my response.

'Mister?'

I turned to see the girl who had been making Edgar's sandwich. She was barely out of her teens, and was gazing at me in utter discomfort.

'Would you like mayo on that?' she asked.

As simple a question as it was, I suddenly didn't know what to say.

Chapter 14

H ugh was trying to stop laughing.

'And you just brought the food down to him and sat there while he ate it?' he asked, tears streaming down his face.

'What else could I do? I had the usual conversation with him about appropriate places to disclose. But you know, probably better than me, that such considerations do not weigh heavily on Edgar's shoulders.'

Hugh produced a pocket handkerchief and wiped his eyes. 'Oh, I'd have liked to have seen that,' he said. 'That's priceless.'

I sipped the glass of iced water he had brought me. I hadn't asked for one, this time, but it seemed that, in Hugh's orderly world, it was now my drink. 'There is the small consideration of the actual disclosure, though, Hugh,' I said. 'We discussed on my last visit the likelihood that Edgar may have experienced sexual abuse. Here we have an open report of just that. Shouldn't we do something about it?'

Hugh sat up and tried to straighten his face. 'Of course. Quite right. It's just that ... well ... has it occurred to you that all he was trying to do was embarrass you?'

I paused with the glass halfway to my mouth. 'What?'

'You'd just had a conversation with him in which you very firmly laid down some clear boundaries,' Hugh said, 'and you refused to be manipulated by him. You mirrored back at him the very abusive way he had dealt with Bridget and me earlier that day. I know Edgar, and he was never going to allow that to stand. I think, my dear Shane, that you have been played.'

I shook my head. 'That may well be the case, Hugh, but we have to work on the premise that the disclosure is genuine. Would you like me to talk to Melanie about it? She's Edgar's social worker, isn't she?'

Hugh nodded, but he still had that soft, pitying expression on his face. He was sure I had been duped, and there was nothing I could say or do that would alter that.

———

I called Melanie when I got back to the office, but only got her voicemail. It was almost ten o'clock that night before she returned my call. When she did, her speech was slurred and she seemed to be only half listening to me. After two minutes of struggling to talk to her over what sounded like jungle music in the background, I gave up.

'Look, Mel, I'll talk to you tomorrow, okay? This is obviously a really bad time.'

'He talked to you, though, di'n't he?' she said. 'He, like, opened up to ya.'

I sighed deeply. 'I don't know if he did or not. Hugh reckons he was only trying to embarrass me.'

'No. De'f'n'y not. You a good worker, Shane. Damn good. Hugh should be d'ligh'ed you're on th' case.'

I shook my head. Melanie was pissed. This was not the right time to be having any kind of conversation with her. 'Look, I'm going to let you go. You're obviously busy.'

'Busy partying on down, baby,' she said, and started to giggle. 'You wanna come party with me?'

'No, thank you,' I said, cringing. 'I'm going to hang up now.'

And I did.

Chapter 15 ∾

Karl Devereux was in his early forties, with long black hair which he wore combed straight back from his angular, clean-shaven face. Today he was wearing black jeans, a grey linen shirt and a brown, soft, leather jacket. I sat in his spartan office, and told him about the Tomescus.

Devereux was an ex-career criminal: he had dabbled in everything from loan-sharking and leg-breaking to assassination and explosives work for a variety of criminal groups, before he had been framed by one of them and served an eight-year stretch in Mountjoy. He now dedicated his life to voluntary youth and community work, mostly in the city's poorer areas where he had grown up.

Most professionals found him unsettling to deal with because he carried a kind of latent threat—a capacity for violence and mayhem that seemed to ooze from him. It was present in the way he moved with a sort of balletic grace borne from years of physical confrontation. It was obvious in the economy and formality of his speech, a result of his time in prison where a careless word can get you killed. Yet I believed him to be a changed man, who was now deeply committed to making a positive difference in the lives of those whom society had turned its back on. He had helped me on a number of occasions, and I trusted and liked him.

'So the husband made himself scarce?' he said, when I had finished speaking. 'It would seem to me that he has implicated himself as the prime suspect. Why not just leave it to the police?'

'I've already given them a statement,' I said, 'but something about the whole thing doesn't sit well with me.'

'What?'

'He told me he didn't do it. She told me he didn't do it.'

Devereux said nothing, his thin lips pursed together, an implacable expression on his face.

'I think I believe them,' I finished.

'And why, pray tell, do you feel you can take the word of a known criminal, whom you have only spoken to for a few short minutes, during which time he threatened you?'

'You're a known criminal. I trust you.'

Devereux put his feet up on his desk. He wore plain black shoes that had been polished to a high sheen. 'I am an ex-criminal. It's not quite the same thing. What do you want, Shane? Why are you here?'

'I want to know which gang Petru Tomescu is involved with.'

'At which level? The gang who trafficked him here? The gang he runs with now? The gang he pays rent to?'

'Is it that complicated?' I asked.

'Yes. He could be mixed up with half a dozen different organisations. How will this help you?'

'I'm guessing he's on the run now.'

'Probably.'

'The gang will know where he is.'

'Maybe. Maybe not.'

'Karl, I don't have anywhere else to look, just at the moment,' I said, exasperated. 'Elvira has asked me to try and find him. I told her I'd do my best.'

'And what possible good will that do?' Devereux said. 'You'll find him, you'll hand him over to the police. If they decide not to deport him or put him in prison, he'll go back to his family, and the domestic violence will continue. This child you've taken on, Litovoi, will be the primary victim. Look at what has been done to him already. Do you want that?'

'You know I don't. But I really believe Petru is innocent of the physical abuse,' I said. 'When I met him in the hospital, I don't think he was threatening me at all. I think he was telling me that he was planning to seek revenge on the people who had hurt his son.'

Devereux nodded. 'Perhaps.' He stood up and walked to the small window of his office. It looked out on to a car park. Across the street was a school that was more prefab than actual building. 'This is a nasty world you are proposing to enter, Shane. These are not good people. Your Petru, even if he didn't beat the boy, would kill you in the blink of an eye without the slightest remorse. There may be some kind of code of honour among the Eastern European gangs, but I have yet to discern quite what it is.'

'Petru seemed to indicate the code was basically "an eye for an eye",' I suggested.

Devereux laughed. 'I think that is a very simplistic representation. I have seen many eyes plucked out without reason or provocation.'

I shrugged. 'I understand all that,' I said. 'I don't want to marry the guy. I just want to find him and bring him back to his family. Elvira told me he's in serious trouble, and I'm not in a position to argue. Can you help me?'

Devereux remained very still at the window. I wondered if he was looking at something, or if he was just standing there for want of anything else to do. The silence stretched out interminably. I hardly knew this man, and there was a gulf between us in terms of life experience, personal beliefs and motivation, yet we seemed to be drawn to one another. For a moment, I wondered what that said about me.

'I can find out which gang he is most involved with,' Devereux said, after a time. 'I can introduce you. But, be warned—dabbling in such things always carries a price.'

'All I want to do is ask them, to try to explain—'

'And if they tell you where to find him, you will be in their debt,' Devereux snapped. 'And believe me, Shane: they *will* collect. It could start out as something small, something easily within your powers to accomplish—a family in need of support, a child assisted in some minor way, but it will escalate, and you will be sucked deeper and deeper into their world. Do you want to run that gauntlet because of a promise you made to a woman who means nothing to you?'

'I'm not some stupid kid, Karl,' I said, trying to speak gently, although I was insulted by his tone. 'I don't look at these people and see modern-day Robin Hoods taking on the system for the good of the common man. I see criminals. I see thugs who trade in human misery and pain. If I can find out from them where Petru is, well then—good. I'll go and talk to him, and see if I can't bring him back to his wife and son. At some time in the future, if one of his associates comes to me looking for help that is within the bounds of my influence and experience to give, I don't care if they see that as being some kind of payment owed because they helped me. If I think they need help, and I can help, then I will. But I will not be pressured into doing anything I disagree with, or that is illegal, or that compromises what I do and who I am.'

'They can bring a tremendous amount of pressure to bear,' Devereux said. 'I'm not sure you realise that.'

'Oh, I do.'

'And how do you propose to deal with such methods of persuasion?'

I grinned. 'Well, I've got you, haven't I?'

Devereux raised an eyebrow quizzically, and then burst out laughing. I had never seen him laugh like that before. It was a little bit unnerving.

'You are a smart man, Shane,' Devereux said. 'If this is a course of action you are set upon, I will do what I can to assist you. We'll deal with whatever opposition we encounter as we encounter it.'

'Thank you.'

'I'll need some information, if I am to proceed.'

'Name it.'

'I need the names, or aliases, of the people the Tomescus are paying money to,' Devereux said, 'and whoever Petru is claiming to work for at the moment.'

'I'll ask Elvira.'

'She will not be happy about telling you, but you need to make her understand that you need the information to proceed—and that you may have to pass what you learn on to the authorities.'

'Sometimes, I think she sees me as the authorities,' I said, sheepishly.

'She would not have asked you to look for Petru if she believed that,' Devereux said. 'She must trust you, at some level.'

'It's my winning smile and sparkling personality,' I said.

'Or perhaps it is just a sign of utter desperation,' Devereux suggested without a hint of irony.

'Well, it could be that,' I admitted.

Chapter 16 ∿

Gregor Blerinca was a short, stocky man, probably in his late sixties, whose bald head glistened under the electric light of his restaurant kitchen. He was chopping leeks as he spoke to us, the heavy, carbon-steel knife rising and falling as if it were independent of his control. Devereux stood just behind me, his hands crossed in front of him as if in prayer. I had sensed a difference in him the moment we walked through the front door of Blerinca's establishment, as if he were picking up a scent that was not perceptible to me. He had spoken to the Romanian fluently, in the little man's native tongue (he told me on the journey over that he had 'done some work' for Blerinca in the past, and had 'picked up a few words'). There was something in each man's eyes, a shared understanding. I wasn't sure I liked it.

'Why you think I can help you find Petru?' Blerinca asked me. 'I am a businessman. He do some kitchen work for me, but yesterday, he no come in to work. If he come back now, I tell him he sacked. It not good to behave in such a way in restaurant trade. You must be dependable.'

There was a quality about him that was staged. I guessed his English was far better than he was letting on. I was seeing the stereotypical image of the poor Romanian immigrant, trying to forge a living from the cruel, uncaring Irish landscape. But it was a performance; Gregor Blerinca was very much in control.

'Petru's wife thought you might know where he is,' I said. 'She suggested that her husband may have done a little more than washing-up for you from time to time.'

The rise and fall of the knife slowed. The Romanian's brown

eyes rose to look at me. 'Say what you mean, sir,' he said. 'What is "more than washing-up"?'

I shrugged. 'You tell me, Mr Blerinca. I don't want to make trouble for you. I just want to know where Petru Tomescu is, so I can reunite him with his family.'

'You do not understand what is going on,' Blerinca said, slamming the point of the knife into the thick wooden board he was using. 'Petru will come home when he can, if he can. Elvira and the boy are safer with him gone. Surely you see that? They only broke the boy a bit this time. Next time, they kill him.'

'Who?' I asked. 'What *is* going on?'

Gregor Blerinca looked over my shoulder at Devereux. '*Pot pot eu să îl încred în?*'

'*Dus putepi să mă incredepi în,*' Devereux said.—'You can trust me.'

Blerinca's eyes narrowed. 'You vouch for him?'

Devereux remained where he was, completely motionless, but his energy filled the low-ceilinged room. 'Of course. I would not have brought him here, otherwise.'

The Romanian nodded. 'Yes,' he said, 'I understand.' He wiped his hands on a dishcloth that was hanging from his belt, and motioned with his head. 'Come, please.'

We followed him through a set of swing doors into the main dining room. He indicated for us to sit at a table, and went to peruse a wine rack. After a few moments, he came to our table, carrying a dusty bottle of red wine. 'This is a 2000 cabernet, from the Uricani vineyard, near Moldavia. It is very, very good. You have some.'

'*Mulțumesc,*' Devereux said.

Blerinca took a corkscrew from his pocket and deftly opened the bottle.

'You must let it breathe,' he said. 'Do not taste it yet, eh?'

The wine had a deep ruby colour. I did as I was told, and let it sit.

'Petru is a good man,' Gregor Blerinca said. 'I knew him when he was just a boy, back in the old country. He was always wild, but he had a good heart. I tried to give him jobs to do around the restaurant, some money in his pocket—instil in him a sense of pride. Children need that. Don't you agree?'

'Yes,' I said. 'Pride in yourself is important.'

'But he was always getting into trouble. He would fight with other boys—bigger boys than he was—and get hurt. When he began to get involved in my ... other ... business, he got into even worse trouble.'

'What kind of trouble?' I asked.

Blerinca smiled at me, but it was the kind of smile a cat might give a mouse. 'My business is far reaching,' he said. I noticed that the clumsy, stumbling delivery had gone. His English had become fluent all of a sudden. 'Petru was involved in the less hospitable aspects of it.'

'Organised crime,' I said.

Gregor Blerinca tutted and shook his head. 'Those are harsh words for what I do. Why must you be so vulgar?'

'I am tired of beating about the bush,' I said. 'You are a gangster, Mr Blerinca. Petru Tomescu is one of your soldiers. I don't know at what level, and I don't want to know. I just want to find him.'

'What people like you, Mr Dunphy, do not understand, is that life is not such a simple thing. Finding a man like Petru is not easy.'

'Why not?' I asked. 'You just tell me where he is.'

Blerinca picked up his wine glass and sampled the nose. 'I am at war,' he said. 'For the past five years, I have been engaged in conflict. I was one of the first to come to this country. I set up my restaurant and I gradually established myself here. I negotiated with your native businessmen. I fought where I needed to fight, I sat still and watched where observation was required. I am not greedy, so I took a little at a time. I was patient. Now, I have many men—some of them are even Irish—working for me.'

'An equal-opportunity employer,' I said.

'Yes. Precisely. You see, I do not care where you were born, or what is your first language. I need good workers, men who are not afraid to get their hands dirty, if there is a need. I pay well, and I ask only for loyalty.'

'Is Petru loyal?' I asked.

Gregor Blerinca sighed. 'Try your wine. It should be good to drink, now.'

We all sampled the cabernet. It was rich and sweet and savoury all at the same time. I had never tasted anything quite like it.

'It is delicious,' I said, raising my glass in a toast to our host.

'Yes, it is a unique wine,' Blerinca said. 'You asked me if Petru is loyal. That is not an easy question for me to answer. I love him as if he was my own son. I know that, in his head, he is always trying to do what is the best thing for me and my interests. But he is a hothead. He is impulsive. Sometimes, he acts before thinking, and that has meant trouble for both me and him.'

'What kind of trouble?' I asked.

'Petru was engaged in some espionage,' Gregor Blerinca said. 'He had infiltrated the ranks of one of my aggressors, and was feeding me back information.'

'Did you ask him to do this?' I asked.

Blerinca shook his head. 'No. He began it without my permission. I started to wonder how he knew so much about what my main competitor was doing. When I finally learned the truth, it was too late. What could I do?'

'So you asked him to continue?'

'It was not a matter of choice. If he had stopped, drawn back, they would have known, and killed him outright.'

'But they did find out,' I said.

'I am not sure, as yet, but I suspect so.'

'Elvira told me she thought the men who attacked her were looking for money. Is that a possibility?'

Blerinca had more wine, and thought about it. 'Did they search her home? Take anything?'

'She didn't say so.'

'Men looking for money for rent or as part of a debt would not have left empty-handed,' Devereux said. 'They would have turned the place over until they found some cash, and if they found none, they would have taken the television, or some furniture to sell.'

I thought about the brand new sofabed. Elvira would have told me if they had taken that.

'Beating the boy was a way of sending Petru a message,' Blerinca said. 'They know about him, and they are angry. They wish him to hand himself over.'

'And by hurting Litovoi, they know he will want to find them, to exact his revenge,' I said.

Gregor Blerinca nodded. 'You are learning,' he said. 'Very good.'

'So what will he do?' I asked. 'Will he give himself up to them out of some twisted sense of honour?'

Blerinca shrugged. He looked at Devereux again. 'What would you do, my friend?'

Devereux had been swirling the dark red liquid about the glass. He sipped some and put it back down on to the table. 'As my captain and benefactor, I would ask you to place some men near my home to ensure my family were protected,' he said.

Blerinca nodded.

'I would know from my wife's descriptions who the assailants were,' Devereux continued, 'and I would hunt them down and kill them. Then, I would seek out the man who had ordered the attack, and kill him.'

Gregor Blerinca looked at me. 'There you have it,' he said. 'In a nutshell, as you might say.'

'He has to be sleeping somewhere,' I said. 'Where is he holed up?'

'That, I do not know,' the Romanian said. 'It is better that I do not. If I do not know, I cannot be made to tell.'

'Plausible deniability,' I said.

'That is a good phrase,' Blerinca said.

'Who would know?'

'He does not have much money,' Blerinca said. 'He might be sleeping rough.'

'If not?'

'Have you talked to the man from whom he rents his flat?'

'No.'

'That is where I would go next, if I were you,' he said.

Chapter 17 ~

Paudy Hennessy was dressed in a blue suit with a narrow pinstripe that might have fitted him in 1982, but now looked as if it was trying to choke the life out of him. He was a sweaty, fat man, with untrimmed, greying sideburns and an untidy moustache. He sat behind his desk in a grubby office below a second-hand furniture store that he also owned. The office had bare floorboards, the paint on the walls was cracked and peeling, and a calendar, which depicted topless models from the *Sun* newspaper, was the only decoration. He had a folder with photographs of various properties in front of him.

'I'm not sure I should be tellin' youse guys anythin' about Mr Tomescu's business,' he said, looking at us. 'Client confidentiality, boys, d'yiz get me drift?'

'You're not a lawyer, Mr Hennessy,' I said. 'Petru is missing, and possibly in some trouble. His wife wishes us to locate him.'

'Listen, bud, if some fella wants to run out on his missus, who am I to argue? Jaysus knows, I've often thought about doin' it meself.'

I looked at Devereux, who had fixed Hennessy with a hard stare. 'Paudy, you have already indicated to us that you have rented Petru Tomescu a room.'

Hennessy seemed to quail for a moment. 'No, I didn't!'

'Yes, you did,' I agreed. 'If you hadn't, you'd just have said "no". Instead, we've been sitting here for the last five minutes while you blew smoke up our arses. Now, do you want to help us out or do we go back to Gregor Blerinca and tell him you've been messing us about?'

Hennessy snorted. 'Blerinca don't scare me none. I'm bein' looked after, and he can't fuckin' touch me. So you can go back and tell him I said he can swivel for all I care.'

Devereux cleared his throat. 'Forgive my associate,' he said, giving me an evil look. 'What he meant to say was that Mr Blerinca would take it as a personal favour if you were to assist him in this small way.'

'I already told yiz, I don't give a fuck about Gregor fuckin' Blerinca or the horse he rode in on,' Hennessy said. 'Youse are wastin' my time. Now git, before I call security.'

'Petru Tomescu has a young son, who is in hospital at the moment. He is asking to see his father,' Devereux said. 'No one needs to know you told us where he is. Please. You would be doing a good thing.'

The fat man sighed, shook his head, and looked pointedly at me. 'You catch more flies with honey than you do with vinegar, you know what I'm sayin'?'

'Well, that isn't my experience,' I said. 'But I'll take your word for it.'

'I don't have that file here,' Hennessy said. 'I'll have to go upstairs. Don't steal nothin' while I'm gone.'

'We'll try to restrain ourselves,' Devereux said.

When the door was closed, Devereux turned to me. 'Shane, you are out of your element,' he said patiently. 'If Gregor Blerinca had any influence with Hennessy, he would have simply telephoned him and asked for the information. Using his name as a form of threat was not wise. It was a card we should have kept until we had a sense of what kind of man we were dealing with, and where his allegiances lay.'

'Sorry,' I said, meaning it. 'Have I fucked things up?'

'Well, he may be up there looking for the file, as he says, or he could be ringing his superiors to ask them what to do.'

'But if he was with the bad guys, Petru wouldn't have rented a place from him, right?'

'Shane, they're *all* bad guys,' Devereux said wearily. 'Haven't you worked that out yet?'

'Yeah, but Hennessy can't be with the guys who are after Petru. That doesn't make any sense.'

'There is a gang war going on,' Devereux said. 'They might not be after Petru, but they won't mind one little bit if something bad happens to him. We have not only told Hennessy that Petru is missing, we've also mentioned that Gregor Blerinca is looking for him.'

'So?'

'So that indicates he's unprotected just now, and therefore vulnerable. You have just made it a lot more dangerous for Petru than it was before we walked in here.'

'Shit,' I said. 'Can you fix it?'

'Not now. Let's just hope Hennessy is as slippery as he looks. He may wish to earn the good will of Blerinca himself in the hopes of doing some business with him, too. If that is the case, we'll know when he comes back in.'

'How?'

'Wait and see. Here he comes.'

Heavy footsteps could be heard on the stairs, and the door opened, admitting Paudy Hennessy. He was carrying a slim cardboard folder.

'Here we go,' he said, sitting down behind his desk again. 'Youse are lucky that I keep such good records.'

'You collect rent, Paudy,' Devereux said. 'Of course you keep records.'

Hennessy shrugged that one away, and opened the folder. 'Bank Lane, number two two five,' he said.

'A flat?' I asked.

'Bedsit. He's only payin' me fifty euro a week. It's a fuckin' steal, really.'

'Is he sharing it with anyone else?' Devereux said.

'No. I offered him the chance to double up, but he wasn't interested. Very much wanted to be on his lonesome. Funny, that—his people usually don't care. I think they like bein' piled into a room like fuckin' sardines. But there you go, takes all sorts, hah?'

'Thank you,' Devereux said, standing. 'I appreciate your assistance.'

I stood also, extending my hand to Hennessy. He shook with me and then Devereux, remaining seated. 'That's all right, boys,' he said. 'You just remember to tell oul' man Blerinca that I done him a good deed, wha'?'

He fumbled about in a drawer and came out with a creased and stained business card. 'Give him this, will yiz? Tell him to give me a call.'

Devereux nodded solemnly, and we left. When we were out on the street in the early evening, Devereux grinned at me and put the card into an inside pocket. 'You got lucky, Shane my boy,' he said. 'His greed got the better of him.'

'I kind of gathered that.'

Devereux laughed and slapped me on the back. Since this whole thing had begun, he'd become much more expressive. 'Gregor Blerinca was right,' he said. 'You are getting good at this.'

'Jesus, I hope the fuck not,' I said, and followed him back to his Volvo.

Chapter 18

L itovoi was healing dramatically quickly. His arm was in a cast, and his chest had been tightly bandaged, but the nurses were already having difficulty keeping him in bed. Elvira had been sent home, but was spending her days at her son's bedside. I sat on the ward with her as Litovoi and another boy in Bob the Builder pyjamas played with some Lego bricks I'd brought in. I smiled as I watched them. Litovoi spoke very little English, and his playmate spoke no Romanian, but language wasn't proving to be a problem. Play was the only language they needed.

'He seems to be doing well,' I said to Elvira. 'You must be pleased.'

'Yes, I am happy,' she said. 'There is no pain for him, I think.'

'I'm always amazed at how tough kids are,' I said. 'Nothing seems to keep them down for long.'

Elvira said nothing—she just continued watching the children playing.

'I am afraid,' she said.

'Of what?' I asked her.

'That the men who hurt us will come back again.'

'Blerinca has men watching your home,' I said. 'But he doesn't think they'll try again. Not now that Petru is gone.'

'Yes,' she said, and her voice sounded thick with tears. 'My husband is gone.'

'I have an address for him,' I told her. 'I called, but he wasn't there. My friend is keeping an eye on it, and we've passed the information on to the police—but I don't know if he's there much.'

'Thank you for trying to find him,' she said. 'I know it is hard thing for you to do.'

'I'm better at this,' I said, nodding at Litovoi. 'But it's important that he gets his dad back. I'll keep trying.'

'Petru is a good father for him,' Elvira said. 'Petru did not have father when he was a boy. Gregor Blerinca was good to him, but not father. He was lonely, I think, much of the time. Is why he do bad things.'

'That can happen,' I said. 'But he's an adult now, Elvira. He can choose to do something different.'

She was laughing and crying at the same time. 'How can he? We need money. The only way for us to get it is if he work for Gregor again.'

I shook my head. 'Not good enough,' I said. 'There are always other ways. Banks, credit unions ... this is not Romania, Elvira. You came here looking for a different life. You've allowed all the awful things to follow you here. You have to make the change happen, now.'

'I do not know how,' Elvira said. 'How do you do this?'

'I know someone who can help you,' I said. 'When we find Petru, maybe you could talk to him.'

Elvira shook her head. 'Why? It is all the same.'

'No. This man is a teacher. He's done a lot of work with people like you. He understands your situation far better than I do.'

'I don't know,' she said. 'It is hard, Shane. Hard to trust.'

I took her hand, and she didn't pull it away. 'I know. You're a long way from home, and you're in trouble and you're scared. I *can* understand that. But you're not alone. Not any more.'

Elvira took a balled-up piece of tissue from her pocket and wiped her eyes.

'We will see. When Petru comes home, we will see.'

'Okay then,' I said, and patted the back of her hand. 'What say we help those two build the biggest Lego house they've ever seen?'

'Yes,' she said, and we forgot about the awfulness of it all for the rest of the afternoon.

Chapter 19

Melanie and Hugh sat opposite me in the office in Bluecloud, looking uncomfortable. I was more than just uncomfortable. I was angry.

'I'm sorry, Shane, but when I broached the subject of ... of what Edgar told you in the café ... Well, he simply denied he'd ever said it,' Hugh said.

'What am I supposed to do?' Melanie added. 'I can't very well stop the access visits with his mother off the back of a disclosure he has, at best, withdrawn.'

I felt myself bristle at that. 'What do you mean "at best"? Are you suggesting I made the whole thing up? That I've exaggerated what happened? Because I have to tell you, there is an entire shopping centre full of witnesses who can corroborate my story.'

'That may well be so,' Hugh said, trying to mollify me, 'but he is now refusing to acknowledge he said anything of the sort. Look, I have a copy of your report, as does Melanie. We'll just have to keep an ear out for anything else that might pop up, eh?'

'I mean, it's amazing that he felt he could open up to you like that,' Melanie said. 'I don't think that's happened with anyone else.'

'Which makes it even harder to swallow, right?' I said.

'No, which means we need much stronger evidence before we can act on it,' she said. 'Come on, Shane, you know the score with situations like this. It is policy to try and keep parents and children together if at all possible. There have been no negative results from the access visits so far as we can tell, so there's no reason to stop them.'

'I'm not necessarily saying you need to stop the visits,' I said. 'But have you asked Edgar's mother about the disclosure? Checked over past files? Spoken to previous contact workers? I mean, this at least warrants further investigation, surely.'

Melanie shifted on her seat. She looked wretched today—there were dark hollows under her eyes, and her hair, usually lustrous and full-bodied, was tied up roughly in a bun. Her clothes were wrinkled—they looked slept in. 'I will, of course, follow up on all those things.'

'When?' I shot back.

'God, Shane, why are you being such a bitch about all this?' she retorted, and stomped out of the room.

Hugh and I sat in silence for a few moments, letting the reverberations of her exit settle. I was fuming. It was a piece of information that could possibly open up a whole new dimension to this case, and it was being left to gather dust. Edgar was on the fast track to a psychiatric facility, and his first real cry for help was being ignored.

'If she doesn't chase this up, I will,' I said to Hugh, who was looking at his hands in embarrassment.

'Don't be too hard on her,' Hugh said, his voice barely audible. 'I don't think she's well.'

I nodded. There was a huge amount neither of us was saying— this was neither the time nor the place, but we both had an idea what Melanie's problem was. I knew a difficult conversation with her was imminent. But maybe not today.

'Is Edgar in?' I asked.

'Where else would he be?' Hugh said.

'I think I'll go and say hi.'

——— .

The boy was in the garden, sitting on a swing and rocking gently.

His whole body was rigid, and his eyes were blank and fixed before him on a point in space. I walked over and stood by the swing.

'Hey, Edgar,' I said.

'Hello,' he said.

'I hear you told them you never said that thing about your mum and the blowjobs,' I said, tapping a cigarette out of the pack.

Edgar said nothing to that, just continued swinging.

'That's cool, Edgar,' I said. 'I don't mind. I just want you to know—I believed you, and I still do. When you're ready to talk about it, I'm right here, okay?'

Again, no response. I lit my cigarette, and sat on the grass.

'We're going out tomorrow. Any thoughts on what you might like to do?'

'Internet,' Edgar said, without hesitation.

'What, you want to go online?'

'Yeah. Internet.'

'Fair enough,' I said. 'I'll ask Hugh if we can use the computer in his office.'

'No,' Edgar said. 'Go out. I want to go to one of them cafés.'

I shrugged. 'Okay. An Internet café it is. Do you want to look something up?'

'Oliver Plunkett.'

'Really? That's great. He caught your interest, did he?'

'I have his picture on my wall, now,' Edgar said. 'Want to see?'

'Sure,' I said.

———

I had not been in Edgar's room before. It was small and very plainly decorated. There was nothing in it that spoke even remotely of Edgar's personality or interests, except for a bookcase filled with assorted volumes and CDs, none of which seemed to have their sleeves attached, and one picture that he had affixed to the wall over his bed. The picture had been produced on an ordinary, run-of-the-mill photocopier, blown up from an image in a text book.

'Saint Oliver Plunkett,' Edgar said. 'I think he's great.'

'I'm really pleased, Ed,' I said, not quite sure how to feel.

'Now, I can look at him whenever I want,' the boy continued. 'He's right there, the first thing I see when I wake up, and the last thing I see before I fall asleep.'

'And what do the staff think of that?' I enquired.

'They don't mind,' Edgar said. 'I think they're pleased I have a friend.'

'A friend?' I asked.

'Yeah,' Edgar said. 'I talk to him. That way, he won't be so lonely.'

I remembered the conversation we'd had at the church.

'And what do ye talk about?' I asked.

'Oh, just stuff. We talked about you the other day.'

I was flattered.

'Did you?'

'Yes. We decided we're glad you took me along to meet him.'

'That's understandable, I suppose,' I said. 'I mean, you wouldn't have got together at all if I hadn't, would you?'

'No, that's right,' Edgar said.

'And why do you think you like Oliver Plunkett so much?' I asked, genuinely curious.

Edgar stared up at the picture. 'He's like me,' he said, turned on his heel and left me standing there.

I looked at the photocopy for a while longer, genuinely uncertain about what was happening. I had no problem with Edgar becoming devoted to a saint. I had no difficulty with him having an imaginary friend—such behaviour is not uncommon, and for a boy as isolated as Edgar, it would have been a healthy sign. What made me feel just a little uncomfortable was the form in which this phenomenon was manifesting itself.

Portraits of Oliver Plunkett are not hard to come by. In life, he had a stern, intelligent face, framed by long brown hair, and he wore a well-groomed moustache and imperial beard.

But Edgar didn't have a picture of the living saint on his wall. He had made a copy of a photograph of the desiccated head in its glass case. The relic stared out at me from unseeing, lidded eyes, its skeletal features created from thick pixels, blurred and fuzzy. I wondered if my bright idea hadn't been a big mistake, after all.

Chapter 20

I found an Internet café not far from Bluecloud—I thought we might walk there. Edgar, so far as it was possible to tell, was positively raring to go. He had his coat on when I arrived, and was standing in the hallway by the front door. As usual, his face was devoid of expression, but I had a sense of pent-up feverish energy.

'Come on,' he said. 'I want to go now.'

'Okay,' I replied, patting him on the shoulder. 'I'll just tell Hugh that we're off.'

The walk took us fifteen minutes. Edgar said little on the way, seeming to hop from foot to foot in his anxiety to get there.

The café was a small, low-ceilinged room with six terminals. When we arrived, there was no one else there but the manager, a pretty blonde woman with glasses. I paid for us to use one of the computers for an hour, and sat down beside Edgar.

Within two minutes, I realised my companion had absolutely no idea how to use either a computer, or the Internet itself. He seemed hell bent on ignoring me, though, and any offers I made of help fell on deaf ears. Instead, he kept calling the young woman over to assist him with the most mundane tasks. I realised we were in for a long and tedious session when she had to explain, albeit good naturedly, how the mouse worked.

But Edgar, for all his lack of computer know-how, seemed determined to continue, and clumsily trawled through the many pages about his new obsession. It was a good thing we were the only customers, because the boy's method of research involved exclaiming loudly each time a page came up, and then reading it to me in his slow, deliberate manner, often (purposely) misreading certain words and replacing them with very rude ones.

'Oliver Plunkett was *ballsed*—oh, sorry, I mean born—in Meath. His family were part of the *gay* class—no, that's wrong, part of the gentry class. Oliver was sent to *ride someone*—oops, I mean sent to Rome to study ...'

And so it continued. I had been doing this type of work long enough to know that intervening would only cause the problem to escalate even further, so I threw my eyes up to heaven, mouthed an apology to the bespectacled administrator, and hoped he'd get bored quickly.

He didn't. Page after page of text was laboriously pored over, the misreads getting progressively more ribald. Finally, after a particularly colourful play on the sentence: 'The bishop refused to have truck with ...' I'd had enough.

'Edgar, I think it's time to stop,' I said quietly. 'You're being rude, and it hasn't been funny for about twenty minutes.'

We had been in the café for approximately twenty-five minutes.

Edgar chose not to notice my statement, and swung round on his chair, looking for the assistant. 'Excuse me,' he said.

Smiling fixedly, the woman came down to him. 'Yes?'

'I think the mouse thing is broken,' Edgar said.

'Let me have a look,' she said, leaning over him and taking hold of it.

She swished it up and down on its mat, and the arrow on the screen moved accordingly. 'No, see? It works fine.'

'It does too,' Edgar said. 'But while you're down here, I've got something for you.'

The fart sounded as if it had come from somewhere subterranean. It had a full-bodied rumble that seemed to make the windows rattle. I am used to experiencing just about every bodily function it is possible to conceive of in the course of my work, but this blind-sided me. My mouth dropped open, but then the smell began to drift across us like a cloud of noxious gas (which, in fairness, it was), and I closed it again quickly.

The noise had been bad, but the aroma that came from Edgar was far, far worse. It is almost impossible to describe—the English language does not have a word that would do it justice.

The blonde administrator had, to her credit, not batted an eyelid at the raucous sound, but the stench was too much for her, and she began to turn a very definite shade of green. 'Excuse me,' she said, and stood up from her position leaning over the boy.

'That's it,' I said, and stood up too. 'Come on, Edgar. This was a bad idea.'

'What?' Edgar said. 'Was it something I did?'

'I'm very sorry,' I said to the assistant, who was sitting at her counter, looking very distressed.

We left.

———

'That was unnecessary,' I said, as we walked back towards Bluecloud. 'That woman didn't even know you. Why act like that around her? What did you gain?'

I suddenly realised I was talking to myself. Edgar had stopped and was gazing at something on the other side of the road. I walked back, and stood beside him.

'What's up?' I said.

'Look at all the bikes,' he said.

Directly opposite us, on the other side of the road, was a bar called the Duke. Parked on the kerb outside it were five very large, shiny Harley Davidson motorcycles. Through the plate-glass window that fronted the pub, the bikes' owners, dressed in leathers and with more facial hair than I could ever hope to grow, could clearly be seen enjoying their drinks and eating lunch.

Before I knew what had happened, Edgar was no longer beside me. He had crossed over, and was standing right beside a stripped-down 1965 Black Shadow, getting his grubby fingermarks all over the chrome. I wasted no time in running over to him.

'Edgar, that bike doesn't belong to you,' I said. 'You should leave it alone.'

'I'd like a motorbike like this,' he said deadpan. 'It's so shiny.'

'That's because the guy who owns it loves it very much, and takes care of it,' I said nervously. 'Now, come on, let's go back to Bluecloud.'

The bikers were, at this stage, only watching us peripherally. They were well used to their rides attracting attention, and didn't mind a kid like Edgar expressing an interest. One of them, an enormous man with a red and green bandana tied about his head and an impressive handlebar moustache obscuring his mouth, cast a glance through the window and nodded at me. I waved and hissed at Edgar, 'Let's go, okay?'

'Okay.'

Heaving a sigh of relief, I turned my back on the huge machines and began to move away. After ten paces, I checked to see if I was being followed, and saw that, rather than being just behind me, Edgar was now perched atop the Harley.

'Oh shit,' I muttered, and hurried back to where I had left him.

Edgar was making loud engine noises, and, as his feet came nowhere near the pedals, was kicking at the paintwork with his mucky shoes. The bandana-wearing biker was looking pointedly at us now, any sense of indulgence long since dissipated.

'Get off right away, Edgar,' I said, 'before that guy comes out and throws you off.'

'Vroom, vroom,' Edgar said. 'Vroom!' He turned and looked me dead in the eye, for maybe the first time. 'He won't touch me,' the boy said, 'but he'll kill you.'

With that, Edgar produced a fifty-cent piece from his pocket, and held it over his head for a moment, so that there could be no confusion about what he was about to do. Then, as I reached over to try and stop him, he leaned down and began to scratch his name on the paintwork.

The bike's owner looked horrified and disbelieving for a moment, and then stood up.

'That's it, I'm off,' Edgar said, and, hopping off the saddle, high-tailed it up the street with more agility than I would have believed possible in a boy of his ample girth.

I regret to report that I remained standing beside the defaced motorcycle for several more seconds, pondering how I was going to explain to an irate Hell's Angel that my young charge was psychiatrically unbalanced. Finally, and none too soon, common sense took hold, and just as the enraged man emerged from the bar's front door, I sprinted past him, following the rapidly shrinking figure of Edgar, as he made for the distant horizon.

Chapter 21 ❧

N eedless to say, Hugh found the story of my close call with
the bikers even more hilarious than the tale of Edgar's
noisy disclosure in the café. I sat in his office and let him
laugh until he cried, then excused myself and went home.

It was a warm spring afternoon, with the sun hanging low in
the sky, so I put on my sweats and went for a run along the river,
before stopping off at the gym and doing weights for an hour.
Feeling refreshed and slightly more positive about the world, I
walked back to my apartment and had a long shower.

I made myself a toasted-cheese sandwich, opened a bottle of
beer, and put a John Coltrane CD on the stereo. I'd enjoyed getting
reacquainted with *David Copperfield* while at the hospital, and
had decided to finish the book so, with *Giant Steps* ringing
pleasantly in my ears, I accompanied Daisy as he visited Little
Em'ly and forgot momentarily about anything else.

———

I must have fallen asleep, because when I awoke Coltrane was
silent as death. The room was in semi-darkness, the book was
open across my chest and my mobile phone was ringing sharply.
I fumbled for it and squinted hazily at the screen. The words
'Melanie' and 'Moorehouse' flashed up at me from the display.
The time winked below the name: 01:30 a.m.

'Mel, what the fuck is going on?' I said tetchily.

All I could hear for several long moments was white noise.

Then the static formed into mingled voices, traffic and footsteps.

'Melanie, are you there?'

I strained to hear against the background sounds and, eventually, she spoke, 'Shane?'

I could tell right away that she was blind drunk. 'What is it, Melanie? It's the middle of the fucking night. I should hang up and go right back to sleep.'

'No, don' hang up the phone,' she slurred. 'Please don' do that. I'm ... I'm in trouble, Shane.'

'What kind of trouble?'

'Can you come and get me?'

I heaved a deep sigh. I was still only half awake, and the better part of my brain was urgently telling me to go to bed without any further delay. But Melanie was my friend, and she sounded terrible. I knew I wouldn't sleep; I'd toss and turn until daylight worrying about her. I stood up and went into the kitchen to get some water.

'Where are you?' I asked as I opened the fridge door and got out a bottle.

'I ... I don' know.'

I took a deep swallow. 'Where were you drinking tonight, Mel? What pub did you go to?'

There was a pause. A siren wailed somewhere behind her, and I heard a voice raised in alarm, shouting something in a language I couldn't understand. 'I can' remember. I'm scared, Shane. Will you come and get me?'

'Yes, I'll come,' I said, taking the keys from their hook beside the kitchen door and grabbing my coat, 'but you need to tell me where you are. I can't get you if I don't know where to go.'

'I don' know.' She was sobbing now. 'I've never been to this place.'

I closed the front door of the apartment building and walked quickly to where the Austin was parked. 'Look around you. Tell me what you can see.'

I could hear her harsh breathing in my ear, and more shouting and engine sounds. 'Shops,' she said at last.

'Can you tell me the names of any of them?'

'Baileys.'

'Is that a pub or a store?'

'I don' know.'

'Can you see anything else?'

'A kind of fountain thing.'

I thought for a moment. A fountain—there were several in the city.

'Look at it a bit more closely,' I said. 'Is there the statue of a swan in it?'

'Hang on a sec.' I heard shuffling footsteps. 'Yeah. There's a white swan in the wa'er.'

The swan fountain was in Bridechapel, on the other side of town. I started the car.

'Right, I know where you are. I want you to stay by that fountain. There's a bench right next to it. Sit down and talk to no one. Okay?'

'Alrigh'. Will you hurry up, please?' She sounded like a little girl. I was already regretting my tone with her, and the row we'd had earlier in the week. Something was going badly wrong for Melanie, and it was more than just her inability to handle Edgar.

'I'll go as fast as I can,' I assured her, speaking gently. 'Just sit tight. I'm going to hang up now. I'll see you very soon.'

'Okay.'

There was no way that I could get from my apartment block to Bridechapel in less than twenty minutes, even in the light night traffic. I just hoped she'd manage to remain unmolested during that time.

I kept (barely) within the speed limit, ran the occasional red light and pulled up at the swan fountain as the clock on my dashboard read five to two. There were very few people about: a wino was slumped in a shop doorway, nursing a crumpled flagon of cider; a young couple were holding one another up in a bus shelter. I could just make out the shape of Melanie on the bench.

To my surprise, I found she was actually asleep, her chin on her chest. I shook her shoulder gently.

'Hey, Melanie. Come on, now.'

She started with a jump, grabbing me by the collar with alarming strength.

'Melanie, it's me!' I felt her grip relax as she realised where she was and that I had come for her.

I helped her to her feet and half carried her to the car. When we reached it, she sat on the passenger seat, her legs still on the pavement and her head in her hands.

'I think I'm gonna be sick,' she said thickly.

I put a bottle of water in her hand and sat behind the wheel. 'Take your time,' I said. 'I'm not in a hurry.'

I put on an Anne Briggs tape at low volume, and sat back. After a few minutes, I heard her retching and saw her shoulders heave. I felt sorry for her. I knew the feeling, and was aware of the sense of self-disgust that goes along with it. But I also realised there was nothing I could say or do to help her until the nausea had passed and she was sober enough to think straight.

'Take some water, Mel,' I said.

'Okay.'

I waited some more. She vomited again. Anne Briggs sang about a tangled man. Slowly and painfully, Melanie sat fully into the car and closed the door.

'Feeling a bit better?' I asked her.

'Yeah ... I think so.'

I started the engine. 'Where do you live?'

Silence. I tapped a rhythm on the wheel. It was a pretty straightforward question, I thought. 'Melanie, what's your address?'

'Can I stay with you tonight?'

I turned to look at her. Her black hair was a tangle of knots and hung lank and greasy. Her make-up, usually expertly applied, was smudged and smeared. A trail of snot ran across her upper lip. Her clothes were rumpled and soiled.

'Why?'

'I don't want to go home. I'm afraid.'

I considered that. 'What of?'

Her voice caught and tears began to stream down her face. 'Of being by myself.'

I reached over and took her hand. 'You can have the spare room tonight, okay?'

She nodded, wiping her eyes with her cuffs, which were already grubby.

'Do I need to take you to a hospital or anything? Are you hurt?'

'No. I'm all right now.'

'You're sure?'

'Yes.'

'Okay, then.'

I had to pull my hand away to release the handbrake, and she reached for it as soon as we were in the flow of traffic. I drove home like that: one hand on the wheel, the other stopping Melanie from tumbling into a pit of darkness from which she might not emerge.

Chapter 22 ~

I took a loaf of wholemeal bread from the oven and set it on a rack to cool, then cracked four eggs into a bowl, added a little milk, chopped parsley and salt and pepper, and whisked the mixture briskly. I had a pan heating on the stove, and, stirring as I did so, slowly poured the eggs into it, watching as they began to solidify. I turned down the heat and continued to stir and fold them until I was satisfied they had reached the desired consistency. Then I transferred them to a bowl and brought them to the breakfast table.

I had already set the table with knives and forks, and there was a jug of fresh orange juice and a cafetière of coffee waiting for someone to push the plunger down.

I heard the shower switch off in the bathroom, and knew Melanie was nearly ready to rejoin the land of the living. I reasoned she could still be some time, so I depressed the plunger and poured myself some coffee.

Ten minutes later, she came unsteadily into the kitchen, wearing a pair of my socks and wrapped up in my dressing gown.

'How's the head?' I asked.

'Don't ask.'

'Okay. Can you stomach breakfast?'

'What've you got?'

'I made some scrambled eggs; a loaf of fresh bread.'

'I'll try, but I'm not promising I'll keep it down.'

'Your loss,' I said, and cut us both a slice of bread and dished out the eggs.

She sat looking at the plate for a time, clutching her coffee cup in both hands as if she needed the warmth, although it was not cold in the room. I ate, half reading the morning paper, waiting for her to offer an explanation for the previous night's episode.

'They'll get cold if you don't eat them now,' I said.

She smiled weakly and picked up her fork. 'I usually grab a takeout coffee at eleven, maybe a pink Snack bar to go with it.'

'This is better for you,' I ventured.

She nodded and took a bite. 'Mmm, good,' she said, but I could tell she was struggling with it. I poured her a glass of juice.

'The vitamin C helps kill the toxins in the blood,' I said. 'Or so I'm told.'

She sat back in her chair, rubbing her eyes.

'I'm sorry about last night,' she said at last. 'I don't know what happened to me.'

'You got drunk and had a blackout, I think,' I said.

'Yeah—I suppose that about sums it up,' she said, looking down at the rapidly congealing eggs on her plate.

'Mel ...' I took a deep breath. 'I've noticed that you've been ... um ... drinking kind of heavily lately.'

'Have you?' she said.

'It would have been impossible not to,' I said. 'You haven't been hiding it very well.'

She laughed dryly. 'Not very classy, huh?'

'I don't think that has anything to do with it,' I said. 'You're obviously going through some stuff ... maybe you need to talk to someone.'

She shook her head and sniffed, blinking back tears. 'It's not that easy.'

'Why not?'

'Shane, this is what I do—I'm a social worker, I help people. I'm not the one that needs fucking help. I mean, I wouldn't even know how to start.'

'I'm not saying it would be a walk in the park. But you can't keep going like this. You'll lose your job, or make some major fuck-up that results in somebody getting hurt. How often are you having liquid lunches, Melanie? Are you driving to your next appointment after them?'

She didn't answer.

'I mean, Jesus, Mel, you're not that stupid. That's beyond reckless.'

'I don't need you lecturing me, Shane. Mr Fucking Perfect.'

'You don't need me lecturing you,' I spluttered, angry now. 'Who did you fucking ring when you regained consciousness lying in a gutter? You knew I wouldn't just pick you up, dust you off and send you on your way. Our friendship has never been like that. You called me because you knew I wouldn't take your crap.'

'I called you because yours was the first number I could actually see, that's all. Don't flatter yourself, arsehole.'

I looked at her, sitting across from me, her cheeks flushed with temper, tears drying on them, her lips pursed. I should have known talking to her wouldn't be easy. We had always sparked off one another, right from the first time we met.

'I don't believe you,' I said, standing up and beginning to gather the plates. 'We both know you're full of shit, so there's no point keeping up the charade. Here's what I'm going to do: I've cancelled my meetings for this morning, and I suggest you do the same—you're not fit for human company right now, anyway. I'm just going to hang out here until lunchtime. You can go back to bed, take a bath, watch TV, whatever you want. If you feel like telling me what's really going on for you, I'm available to listen. If you'd prefer to talk to someone else, I have a notebook full of numbers beside the phone. The rest, as they say, is up to you.' I started to scrape the leftovers into the bin.

'Shane,' she said.

'What?'

'Thanks.'

Then she went back to bed.

At midday I was working on some plans for future visits with Edgar. So engrossed was I, I didn't notice Melanie standing over me, fully dressed, her bag on her arm.

'I've called for a taxi—I'll be going in a few minutes,' she said.

I looked up from my laptop. She was wearing no make-up, and still looked hung over and tired.

'Okay,' I said, not sure how to respond after the row we'd had earlier. 'Well ... um ... take it easy.'

She nodded and chewed uncertainly on her lower lip, fiddling with the strap of her bag. 'I'm sorry about how I've been,' she said haltingly. 'I didn't mean for things to get so fucked up.'

'I know that, Mel,' I said. 'You don't need to apologise to me.'

'I do. I need to explain. But it's hard, y'know? There's so much I need to say, but I don't know how to tell you yet. You have to give me some time.'

I went over to her and put my arms round her. 'You know where I am, when you feel ready,' I said. 'You're not alone.'

She held me tightly, then turned and, without another word, walked out the door. I watched her go. There was a lot that needed to be said: that she should ask for some time off work, that she should seriously think about going to AA, that there wasn't anything she was going through that couldn't be sorted out—but I didn't say any of it, just looked at the closed door and felt useless.

I sat back down, saved what I'd been doing, and went to the office. I could just as easily feel useless there, and at least I'd have Mrs Munro for company.

Chapter 23 ~

I'd been playing a Thursday night gig with a multi-instrumentalist named Dave Bligh (a tall, thin, bespectacled character, who favoured baggy woollen jumpers and drainpipe jeans) in a bar called Harper's on the east side of the River Torc. It was a long, narrow, oldy-worldy sort of place that attracted a lot of students and artsy types. What I liked about it, and what was quite unusual, was that many of the people who drank there actually came to listen to music rather than talk loudly over it.

Dave and I played a mixture of folk songs and traditional Irish, Scottish and American tunes, with a bit of jazz thrown in for good measure. My friend liked to state that there wasn't an instrument he couldn't knock a melody out of, and this was not an idle boast. I never knew from one night to the next which combination of oddities he was likely to turn up with: a hurdy-gurdy, an autoharp and a didgeridoo one night, an Appalachian dulcimer, a balalaika and set of kazoos the next.

Dave was well travelled, and everywhere he went he seemed to pick up waifs and strays. Some (though by no means all) of these individuals were fine musicians in their own right, and any time they happened to be passing through the city, they would seek him out and come along to the gig. So, together with his bizarre junkshop orchestra, my partner in musical crime was also likely to arrive with a strangely attired friend carrying an instrument case. Life was never boring with Dave about.

Because of this, I looked forward to our weekly sessions. It was an opportunity to step outside my life as a care worker, completely forget whatever cases were currently on my books, and simply lose myself in the music.

This particular Thursday night was crowded and the air in the bar was heavy with the heat of bodies and the sound of chatter and glasses clinking. Dave and I were in our usual spot just inside the door, which was specially designated in Harper's as the music corner. I rarely travelled without at least three instruments, and Dave could arrive with even more, so we needed a bit of space for our stands, cases and other paraphernalia. When we'd finally settled in, tuned our instruments and got our drinks, we looked at one another expectantly. It's always a moment of strange trepidation, that first song or tune of the night.

'What about a few reels?' I asked.

That evening, Dave had decided to play it safe, and had brought a traditional wooden flute, a two-row button accordion and a beautiful old mandola.

'"Rakish Paddy"?'

'That'll do,' I said.

I chopped out a rhythmic introduction on my guitar, and Dave played the first part of the reel in his sweet yet punchy accordion style. I always loved to watch him play. He would close his eyes, and sway gently to the rapid syncopation of the music, as if being lulled by it. His fingers scarcely seemed to move over the keys, neither did he appear to operate the instrument's bellows much: the melody just flowed from him. 'Rakish Paddy' merged into the second tune in the set, 'The Tailor's Fancy', and I dropped out, allowing him to play the first part solo. This was a trick we did now and again—Dave would slow down slightly, and play the signature melody in a very ornamental, intricate manner, letting each note stand out, and emphasising the hook of the tune. People often argue that traditional Irish tunes all sound the same. This is simply not true, but many musicians play the music so fast that all nuances and differences are lost in the flurry of notes. Dave and I had made a conscious decision when we started playing together to allow the melodies to speak for themselves. For the third and final tune in the set—'The High Reel'—I switched to mandocello and we took off at a fair old pace again, to whoops of appreciation from the audience. We finished the set with a flourish, and nodded our thanks to the cheering crowd.

The night continued merrily. We tended to follow each set with a song, and alternated vocal duties between us. Dave had a pleasant voice, and an eclectic repertoire, so our performances were always varied. At eleven o'clock, we usually slowed things down, and one or other of us would perform one of the great epic ballads from the folk tradition. Many of our regular listeners had told us that this part of the evening was a highlight for them, as such songs are not often played any more. Yet, those who take the time to listen can still find in them all the poetry, beauty and majesty of a great work of art.

This particular evening, as the audience seemed particularly receptive, I decided to sing 'Little Musgrave', a medieval epic that told the story of a knight who falls in love with his lord's wife, and pays the ultimate price. The song has a delicate, lilting melody, and I always find the images running in my head like a film when I sing it. There is a dreamlike quality to the song that I find irresistible.

It fell upon a holy day, as many's in the year.
Musgrave to the church did go to see fine ladies there
And some were dressed in velvet red and some in velvet pale,
But then in came Lord Barnard's wife—the fairest among them
*   all.*
She cast an eye on the little Musgrave, as bright as the summer
*   sun.*
Says Musgrave unto himself: 'This lady's heart I've won.
Oh I have loved you fair lady, for long and many's the day.'
'And I have loved you, me little Musgrave, and never a word did
*   say.'*

The two go to Lord Barnard's hunting lodge, and consummate their relationship, but the lady's page is loyal to his master, and informs him of his wife's betrayal. Barnard goes to the lodge, finds the lovers in bed, and challenges Musgrave to a duel, during which, despite being sorely wounded, Lord Barnard slays his competitor.

> *Then up spoke the lady fair, from the bed whereon she lay:*
> *'Although you're dead, my little Musgrave, still for you I pray.'*
> *Barnard took out his long, long sword, to strike the mortal blow.*
> *Through and through the lady's heart, the cold steel it did go.*
> *'A grave, a grave,' Lord Barnard cried, 'to put these lovers in.*
> *With my lady in the upper part, for she came from better kin.*
> *For I've just slain the finest knight that ever rode a steed.*
> *And I've just killed the finest lady that ever did a woman's deed.'*

We finished the song, me finger-picking the droning two-chord sequence, he playing the pretty signature riff high on the mandola's fret board. As the song ended and applause washed over us, I looked across the sea of faces, and there, standing attentively by the bar, was someone I thought I recognised. I had to do a double-take, because this person's presence was completely out of context but, with my second glance, I saw that I was right: Gregor Blerinca was among the audience that night.

I had no idea if this was purely a coincidence, or whether the gangster was there to cause trouble for me, but I decided to put it out of my mind and simply get on with the business of playing. If Blerinca wanted to speak to me, he knew where I was. And, of course, I was safe as long as I stayed in the very public confines of the pub.

We played our final piece at twenty to twelve. The landlord brought us over two pints of Guinness, congratulated us on a great night of music, and left us to chat.

'I've just picked up an old Stroh violin,' Dave said, rolling a cigarette. 'It needs some work—it hasn't been played in donkey's years, but there's still a really good sound out of it.'

I checked the bar, but there was no sign of Blerinca. It must have been a coincidence, after all. 'I've never heard you play the fiddle, Dave,' I said. 'Are you any good?'

'I'm very good,' he said, matter-of-factly. 'I pretty much played nothing else from eighty-one to eighty-five.'

'That's not like you.'

'The learning curve for the violin is fairly shallow. You sound like shit for a very long time. It requires dedication and commitment.'

'The Stroh violin—that's the one with the metal sound resonator, isn't it—like on an old gramophone?'

'That's it. I'm hoping to have it in working order in a month or so.'

'Where'd you come across that then?' I asked, accepting a roll-up from him. 'They're quite unusual these days, aren't they?'

'They still use them in a lot of German folk music,' Dave conceded. 'And a lot of Eastern European bands have them. As you can imagine, a glut of the things have arrived in Ireland over the past few years.'

I was about to respond, when I felt a hand on my shoulder—a firm, resolute grip. 'Mr Dunphy, would you be so good as to have a brief chat with me—privately?'

I recognised the voice immediately. Gregor Blerinca had not left the bar, after all.

———

We sat outside in the smoking area. I had asked the landlord if he minded us staying while he and the rest of the staff cleaned up, so we had the place to ourselves.

'What can I do for you, Mr Blerinca?' I asked.

He sipped from a glass of whiskey. 'I enjoyed your music very much. The song about the knights and the lady—we have many songs like that in the old country. Songs of honour, songs of death.'

'I'm glad you liked it. I tend to think of it more as a love song, but I suppose it's about honour and death, too.'

'You play well. Maybe you could come and play at my restaurant, eh?'

'I don't know any Romanian songs, I'm afraid.'

He laughed at that. 'No, I don't suppose you do.'

'Did you come here tonight to listen to me play, Mr Blerinca, or was there another reason?'

'You are right,' he said. 'We should get to business. I helped you, a few days ago, yes?'

I shrugged. 'A little.'

He nodded. 'I could be of more assistance.'

'How?'

He sat back, looking about him to make sure no one was eavesdropping. 'You work with children, Mr Dunphy, do you not?'

'Yes.'

'Do you, as part of your job, help parents whose children are not behaving as they should?'

I scratched my head. 'That's not how I would have put it, Mr Blerinca, but I suppose I do, from time to time. It's called "behaviour management". Of course, I would always ensure that any plan to alter a child's pattern of behaviour is good for the child, not just the parent.'

Blerinca narrowed his eyes at me. 'Parents know what is best for their children, Mr Dunphy.'

'In my experience, sadly, they do not always have their children's best interests at heart.'

He did not seem to know how to respond to that, and sipped from his whiskey some more, instead.

'I have a son, Mr Dunphy. Vladimir. He is sixteen years old.'

I waited. He drank. I knew he was searching for the way to say what he needed to say that would hurt him the least.

'I want you to understand—I love my son a great deal. I was too old when he was born. I could not, or perhaps I was not so inclined—I am man enough to admit it—to do some of the things a father should with a young boy: sporting activities, rough and tumble—manly things. As a result, he has grown to be ... um ... sensitive. Gentle.'

'Isn't that good?'

'No. It is not good. One day he will succeed me, and then he will have to be strong and tough.'

'And that is a definite eventuality? He must one day take over your empire?'

'Yes. That is how it is done.'

'And what if he doesn't want to follow in your footsteps? He might want to be an actor or a poet or a fashion designer. Wouldn't it be better that he choose his own path in life?'

Blerinca shook his head. 'You do not understand. Even if he does not take an active role in the business, he will *own* everything. There will be many who will wish to take it from him. To withstand that, he must know how to act like a man.'

'Can't he be a silent partner? I'm sure you have other relatives who could take a managerial position.'

'He would still have to make important decisions—order things that would be difficult to take responsibility for. He needs to learn how to do that.'

'And why do you think he won't be able to?'

'I know my son. He is not—how would you say ... he is artistic, and enjoys popular music. He reads magazines.'

'Magazines?'

'Yes.'

I let that one go. The possibilities for what he meant were endless, and I wasn't sure I wanted to follow the line of thought to its conclusion. I stood up. 'I don't think I can help you,' I said.

'There are, as I understand it, lots of different ways to be a man. I don't want to be the one to bully your son into some mode of masculinity he's not comfortable with. I'm sorry.'

I began to walk to the door.

'What do you want?' he called after me. 'I can get you anything. Money, women, drugs—whatever is your wish, I can provide it.'

I stopped, but did not turn to look back at him. 'I am not for sale, Mr Blerinca.'

There was a long moment of silence. I took a deep breath and continued to walk towards the door.

'Vladimir is unhappy,' the old man said, just as I reached it. 'I do not understand such things. I come from a different place and a different time. All I want you to do is meet him. Talk to him. I would like to see him smile again. I only want what is best for him.'

'What if that happens to be something you don't like?'

I turned slowly to look at him. His face was lined with the struggle he was going through. Blerinca was not used to this kind of discussion. 'Please help my son,' he said, urgently.

I went back to the table. 'I want you to understand, Mr Blerinca, that if I see your son, it will only be with the agreement of my boss. This will be above board and by the book. No favours, no under the counter trading. Are we clear?'

He nodded. 'Of course.'

I stood again. 'I'll call you at the restaurant when I have word.'

'Thank you.'

'Thank me after I've met Vladimir,' I said, and left him sitting there, alone with his pain.

Chapter 24

I cradled a cup of instant coffee in my hands, and waited as Elvira Tomescu made me a sandwich. Litovoi, his arm still in a cast, was lying on the floor in front of the TV watching *SpongeBob SquarePants*. I've got to admit that I've never really understood the cartoon. I've read that it is a work of post-modern genius, and is supposed to appeal as much to adults as children, but whatever elements are aimed at my demographic, I have missed them utterly.

'Why is there a squirrel living under water?' I asked Litovoi.

'She is SpongeBob's friend,' the child answered, his tone telling me that he thought the answer obvious.

'And how do they cook burgers? I mean—it just wouldn't work. And what are the burgers made from? Do they have cows on the bottom of the ocean?'

'Sshh!' Litovoi said.

I sipped the coffee and immediately regretted doing so. I don't drink instant, as a rule, because it doesn't taste remotely like coffee. Elvira came in from the tiny kitchen, carrying a cheese and pickle sandwich on cheap white bread. I smiled and took it. 'Thanks. I'm starved.'

'You are welcome.'

I took a bite. It wasn't bad.

'So Petru hasn't been in touch?' I asked.

'No. We miss him, don't we, Craig?'

'Sshh,' Litovoi said.

'I don't know where he is either,' I admitted, 'and the Gardaí are at a complete loss. I think we just have to accept that he'll either come back on his own, or he won't.'

'He might be dead,' Elvira said, plainly.

'I don't think it helps to think like that,' I said. 'We just don't know.'

'It does not help to keep hoping,' Elvira said. 'It makes me too sad. I cannot sleep at night.'

'I wish I could help,' I said. 'I'm sorry.'

'You should not feel sorry,' Elvira said. 'You have been very kind to us.'

'I'll tell you what,' I said. 'Let's do something nice this afternoon. Why don't we go and see a film or something.'

'What do you mean?' Elvira said, looking confused.

'Let's go to the cinema. Watch a movie.'

She shook her head. 'I have no money.'

'My treat. Come on, I feel like seeing something silly. Hey, Litovoi, do you want to come see a film with me and your mum?'

'Yeah!' he said, finally looking up from the bizarre TV show.

'Great, that's decided then. If we leave now, we'll be in time for the three o'clock show.'

'You are crazy,' Elvira said, unable to stifle a smile.

'Sometimes, you just have to go with the flow,' I said, helping her on with her coat. 'Anyway, we all need to have some fun. Doctor's orders.'

'I want popcorn,' Litovoi said as we went out the door to the car.

'Then you shall have popcorn,' I said. 'And ice cream and fizzy drinks and a big bag of those sweets that you have to get weighed and that cost six times as much as normal sweets.'

'Yeah!'

'Craig, you will be sick,' Elvira said.

'That's all part of the fun,' I said, holding open the door of the Austin for her. 'We'll all be sick.'

We spent two hours watching an utterly ridiculous, but nonetheless enjoyable, Disney movie in which a cartoon princess fell down a well and ended up in live-action modern-day New York. This was unbelievable enough in itself, but then the producers pushed the bounds of credibility beyond all reason by having her fall in love with a lawyer. There was, of course, a handsome, square-jawed prince and a wicked witch and a funny computer-generated chipmunk, and it all ended happily.

We didn't get sick, but we did eat far too much rubbish. Elvira had as good a time as Litovoi, if not a better one. It was late evening when I dropped them back home. Litovoi was happy and sleepy, and curled up on the couch. Elvira pulled a blanket over him.

'Thank you,' she said. 'That was a wonderful afternoon. I have not laughed so much in long time.'

'You're welcome,' I said. 'I had a good time, too.'

'I wish Petru could have been with us,' she said, smiling sadly. 'Then would have been perfect.'

I patted her on the shoulder. 'I know. I know, sweetheart.'

Looking back, I wish I'd had something more comforting to say, but nothing occurred to me. Sometimes, words just can't make things better.

Chapter 25

'No, Shane,' Ben Tyrrell, my boss, said. 'I don't think it's in any way appropriate for you to get involved with this man any further. I can understand, although I do not condone, you making contact with him in your efforts to locate Petru Tomescu, but there, I think, it should end.'

We were at the fortnightly team meeting, held in the conference room at Dunleavy House. Ben was a young-looking fifty-four, still slim and wiry of build, with a goatee beard, round wire-framed glasses and longish brown hair peppered with grey. The rest of the group—Marian, Loretta, Jerome and Clive—were seated about us, files and reports spread about them, looking decidedly uncomfortable. I had made an impassioned plea to be permitted to meet Vladimir Blerinca, but it was clear after thirty seconds that Ben was not going to be easily persuaded. In fact, he was quite angry.

'Aren't we in the business of helping people?' I asked. 'There might be nothing wrong, and it'll be wrapped up in no time at all. I can spare a few hours.'

'Shane, this man is a known criminal—you've said so yourself.'

'How many times have we all worked with families involved in crime? It's kind of an occupational hazard in this business, isn't it?'

'You're playing with semantics,' Ben said, and his voice was full of warning now: you're pushing your luck, Shane; back off. 'There is a huge difference between a family being on the periphery of crime and effectively being part of an organised criminal dynasty.'

'I think *that* is a semantic game. I mean, should we be in a position to choose who deserves help and who doesn't? If this boy needs our support, then surely we should extend the hand of friendship. He can hardly be blamed for the sins of his father.'

'Has it occurred to you that this boy's father can well afford to pay for private therapy? Why should we invest our time and skills when there are so many families that cannot afford to access those kinds of services privately?'

'The Tomescus are part of a community, Ben,' I said, trying to keep my voice even. 'One of the reasons people like them have not really integrated is that they have been seen in isolation—single families with individual problems. The way I have tried to address the needs of Litovoi and his parents is to go into the Romanian community and seek support there. The problems that exist for them go right back to their backgrounds in their homeland. We can't see them as a set of difficulties that just evolved when they arrived here—we have to look at their needs holistically.'

'I've been doing this work for a lot of years, and I don't need you spouting a load of buzzwords at me.'

'That's a crock, Ben, and you know it—'

'I'll think about it,' Ben said, and I knew by the expression on his face and the finality of his tone that the discussion was over.

The rest of the team heaved a sigh of relief, and the meeting limped onwards, with Ben and me avoiding one another's gaze for the remainder of the time.

———

When we were finished, I gathered up my paperwork and left the room without saying a word to anyone. I dumped the pile of notes on the desk in my office, and went to get some lunch from the sandwich stand a couple of streets over.

I was on my way back when I saw Ben approaching. I considered crossing the road to avoid him, but decided that was just too childish.

'That got a little tense,' he said, when we came face to face.

'It happens, sometimes,' I said, trying to gauge his mood.

'Would you hang on while I get a bite, and then we can sit and talk properly—no fighting, no one-upmanship, just a proper exchange of ideas. What do you say?'

'That would be good,' I said.

He got a sandwich, and we walked to a bench just across the road from Dunleavy House, which overlooked a duck pond. The sun was pleasant, and the path round the water was busy with people walking small dogs, jogging while listening to MP3 players, or hurrying on their way to lunchtime meetings.

'Why do you want to work with this boy?' Ben asked when we were seated. 'I bet you can think of a hundred reasons not to—I know you're not stupid or blindly idealistic. So what's going on?'

'The old man seemed genuinely upset about him,' I said, taking a bite of my egg salad on wholegrain. 'If I'd thought he wasn't, I'd have just walked away.'

'He might be upset because he's afraid the kid's weak, or disabled, and therefore an unworthy heir. His feelings could easily be totally self-serving.'

'Are anybody's feelings really altruistic?' I asked. 'Most of us see the world through the lens of our own needs and experiences. I'm not going to abandon him because of that.'

Ben took a sip from his green tea. An old drake had waddled up to us and was hanging about, waiting for one of us to throw him a crust. Ben picked a piece of bread off his sandwich and tossed it on the grass just in front of the bird.

'Do you know anything about Blerinca, beyond what Devereux has told you?' he asked me. 'Have you any sense of whether he is even remotely trustworthy? Will he have you beaten or killed if you don't do as he wishes? Can you hope to approach this in a child-centred manner?'

'The first thing I said to him was that the needs of his son may not be what he would like. He seemed to accept it.'

'*Seemed to*—that's not very definite,' Ben retorted. 'Shane, if I'm going to send you out on this case, I need to know you're safe.'

'I will operate the same safety procedures I would with any other: public places, letting Mrs Munro know where I am, having my phone switched on—I can't do much more than that.'

'Gregor Blerinca found out about you playing at Harper's. Do you think he doesn't know where you live?'

I had already thought about that.

'It's no different to any other case, really. We all live and work in the city—I play music, I go to the gym, I drink coffee in cafés and eat in restaurants. We all have lives, and they don't stop because we do what we do. I mean, Jesus, Ben, we've dealt with paedophiles and violent monsters and all kinds of horrible people in the past. Blerinca came to me, looking for help for his son. He says the kid is unhappy. He's not dense. Having me whacked isn't going to make his son any happier.'

Ben nodded. Our food was finished. I took two cigarettes out and gave him one. I sparked my Zippo and held it out for him.

'I'm still not buying it,' he said. 'Why do I get the sense there's more going on in this for you?'

I lit my own smoke and shook my head. 'You don't fucking let up, do you, Ben?'

'I'm not known for it, no.'

I watched the old duck as it sat patiently, waiting for one of us to produce some more edible scraps.

'Maybe what he told me about Vladimir reminds me a little of me when I was that age.'

Ben blew smoke rings in a steady stream, each one perfectly formed. 'I didn't know you had a conflicted relationship with your father.'

'No, I don't mean that. When I was a kid I didn't know where I fitted in. I grew up in a big local-authority housing estate, staunchly working class, but my mother's sensibilities, and therefore my own, were much more middle class. While the other kids were playing football and building trollies, I was doing drama and going to the chess club. I was into writing and music and, because my mum was English, I didn't even speak like the rest of them. Maybe I know what it feels like to be an outsider.'

'So you think that you can kill off your alienation complex by helping young Vladimir.'

I laughed. 'Ben, I'm a man who works with kids for a living. I'm a left-wing hippy folk musician in a hip-hop, Dolce and Gabbana wearing, consumer society. I drive a car that was laughed at even when it was new. I don't think I'm likely to lose my alienation complex anytime soon.'

Ben patted me on the shoulder and flicked his cigarette butt over the duck's head into the pond. 'I'm going to sanction one meeting with Vladimir Blerinca. I want a full report. Then we'll see. That's as much as I can give you today.'

'It's enough,' I said. 'Thanks.'

'Don't thank me yet,' he said, standing up and brushing the crumbs from his lap. 'It could all go tits up yet.'

'Given my track record,' I said, 'it probably will.'

E dgar O'Sullivan sat in the back seat of the Austin and sang Elvis Presley songs tunelessly and loudly. This was another piece of the puzzle that was his personality which I was encountering for the first time. He seemed to have an almost encyclopedic knowledge of the King's back catalogue, and each song would be sung right through from beginning to end, complete with vocal representations of instrumental solos. Each time a song ended and a new one began, Edgar would introduce it by informing the listener (I was a captive audience, but I didn't think he really cared if there was anyone to hear or not) of the year, album and/or movie the song had initially appeared in.

Interestingly, unlike most Elvis fans, he made no effort to mimic Presley's trademark crooning delivery (itself a slightly updated version of Dean Martin), but simply sang the songs very much in his own voice, without apparent pleasure.

'Thank you all,' he said. 'I will now sing for you the 1961 song from that great movie *Blue Hawaii*: "Rock-a-Hula Baby".'

'Thang you verah much,' I said, unable to resist.

Edgar completely ignored me, and began to sing. I was tempted to sing along with him, but decided to let him be. The entire experience could have been extremely annoying, if it hadn't been for the fact that I was intensely curious as to how many songs he would know, and how long the activity would hold his attention. The songs he was choosing were not, to my great puzzlement, the really iconic ones. He did not sing 'Suspicious Minds', or 'In the Ghetto', or 'Blue Suede Shoes'.

Instead, I was treated to 'You Can't Say No in Acapulco', 'Guitar

Man' and 'Devil in Disguise'. It was very strange, and kind of sad. I had an image of chubby, unloved Edgar, closeted away in his bedroom, dozens of Elvis Presley CDs strewn across the floor, his expression manic as he desperately tried to learn the lyrics, his soulless voice awkward as it tried to cope with the soaring melodies. It was a lonely picture.

For me, music has always been something to be shared with others, a form of expression unlike any other in its capacity to capture emotion at both its most joyous and its lowest, darkest ebb. Was I the first person Edgar had shared his love for Elvis with? Was he actually sharing at all? It was impossible to be sure.

We were on our way to meet Edgar's mother, Collette. Despite having been on several access visits to her by this stage, the woman was still a blank slate to me. I knew she had been responsible (if that was even the correct word) for neglecting Edgar terribly. Beyond that, I knew absolutely nothing about her. The staff at Bluecloud reported that the boy seemed to have neither positive nor negative reactions to his meetings with her. He had never spoken of his life before coming into care. I wondered if his interest in Elvis was a new one, or a remnant of his pre-care existence. I made a mental note to try and find out.

'I'm thirsty,' Edgar said, rousing me from my thoughts.

'We'll be there in a few minutes,' I said. 'I was planning on getting something to eat and drink then, okay?'

'I can't wait,' Edgar said. 'I'm really, really thirsty. I need a drink now.'

The sensible part of me wanted to tell him that waiting for ten more minutes would not cause him to expire. The afternoon was, however, still very much in its early stages, and I had learned with Edgar that it was important to pick my battles carefully. This was not an argument it would be useful to pursue.

'There's a petrol station up ahead,' I said. 'I'll get you something there.'

He decided on Coke and, crisis averted, we drove on.

'What's in this bag?' Edgar asked several minutes later, in between slurps and gulps of fizzy drink.

'Oh, it's just work stuff.'

Edgar was referring to a leather satchel in which I kept files, reports and other information that I needed.

'Is it important?'

'Yes, I suppose so.' The words had barely escaped my lips when I realised the mistake I had made. Edgar fell very silent all of a sudden. I tried to catch a glimpse of him in the rear-view mirror, but he shrewdly slid down as low as he could in the seat.

'What are you up to, Edgar?' I asked.

'Nothing.'

'I don't believe you.'

Glug. Glug. Glug.

The sound of liquid being poured from one receptacle into another filled the car. Each glug was accompanied by a gentle fizzing. I could guess what was going on in the back of the car, but decided that commenting on it was precisely what Edgar wanted me to do, so I switched on the radio, and drove on, gritting my teeth in temper.

Edgar's mother lived in a small rented house on a quiet, shady street just outside the city. When I parked, Edgar clambered out in his customary ungainly manner and walked up the front path to the door. I picked up my bag, which sloshed audibly. The Coke can lay empty on the seat, dripping the remainder of its sticky brown contents onto my upholstery. Most of what hadn't ended up inside Edgar, however, was now in my bag, soaking into the paperwork. Gingerly, I held the satchel at an angle and tried to pour the Coke into the gutter. That accomplished, I pulled out a sheet of paper, to see how much damage had been done. It was completely ruined—stained and utterly saturated. I closed the bag, which would now require some form of special treatment by a professional to make it clean and usable again, and put it and its sodden contents into the boot. I then followed Edgar. Most of the damaged papers were copies—the originals of which were in the filing cabinet in my office—but some had been field notes: phone numbers, random thoughts, spontaneous observations I always tried to record so that I could refer to them later. All of these were now lost. At that moment, I could cheerfully have strangled Edgar O'Sullivan.

When I got to the front door Collette was standing waiting for me. She was a short, almost dwarfish woman, round as a beach ball, with very thick glasses balanced on her tiny button nose. Her hair was a kind of dense, light brown afro, which sat in a cloud about her small head. Collette's arms and legs seemed curiously out of proportion to her body—if I had never seen her walking and using a knife and fork, I would have assumed her limbs to be almost vestigial, so short and stubby did they appear.

'So, Shane,' she said, as I held my hand out to shake hers. Collette always seemed to be on the verge of laughter. Her eyes behind the impossibly thick prescription lenses were wide and manic. Life, to Collette, was a joke almost too hilarious to bear. Sentences often terminated with a guffaw or an explosion of giggles. I'm afraid that I am not much good at simulating mirth when I do not see the joke, and Edgar never seemed to laugh at all, so Collette usually ended up chortling away on her own during our visits. 'I have some great news for ye,' she said. Edgar had gone on into the dark little house, and we were alone on the step.

'Oh. What's that, then?' I asked.

'Now, now, you'll just have to be patient, you bold boy, you,' Collette said, swatting at my arm and squealing with hilarity.

'You are a tease,' I said wearily. 'Give Edgar a shout and we'll get going. Have you eaten? I think your son is on the verge of gnawing his arm off with hunger.'

'Well, I had some lunch, but sure I could always eat again. I've never had to worry about my figure. I just don't seem to put weight on.'

'Lucky you,' I said, marvelling at such an alarming lack of self-awareness.

'It's my metabolism, I think. And sure, I'm always on the go,' she said, barely containing her jollity. 'I fancy chips. Will we have some chips, Shane?'

'I daresay we could find somewhere that serves them,' I said.

———

There was a steak house a quarter of a mile up the road, and we got a table there.

'Edgar, Shane,' Collette said, almost bursting with excitement and glee, 'there's something I've been wanting to share with you both for ages now.'

Edgar was shovelling chips into his mouth, and appeared not to hear her. Collette, for her part, seemed not to care. 'Now, I know you're both going to be as happy as I am about this, so I'm going to come right out and say it.'

I waited expectantly. Edgar picked up his burger and began to take huge bites from it, filling his mouth with meat, salad, sauces and bun. Grease ran down his chin in gobs.

'Oh, you've just dragged it out of me, you terrible, terrible chaps,' Collette hooted. 'Well, here goes then—in for a penny in for a pound, as my old mother always used to say. Lads: I'm going to have a baby.'

Edgar crammed in the last of his burger and sat back, chewing mechanically. I looked at the tiny woman, perched opposite me in the restaurant like something that had escaped from a twisted fairy tale.

'Umm ... congratulations ...' I said. 'Isn't that great news, Edgar? You're going to have a little brother or sister.'

Edgar swallowed noisily and reached for the big laminated menu. 'I want ice cream,' he said.

'He's delighted!' Collette said. 'Why don't we all have some ice cream to celebrate?'

I looked down at my untouched steak and salad, and pushed it aside. Somehow, I didn't feel like eating any more.

Chapter 27

H ugh Whitty got off shift that evening at ten o'clock, and I met him on the corner, just down the road from Bluecloud. It was a pleasant, warm night, with a sky full of stars; the orange glow of light pollution caused by the city looked almost pretty over the horizon.

'To what do I owe this pleasure?' Hugh asked as we strolled along well-manicured streets towards the shopping area. It was late opening at the nearest shopping centre, Hugh informed me, and he needed to pick up some odds and ends.

'I take it Edgar didn't mention Collette's bombshell,' I said.

'No. He was his usual immutable self when he got back.'

I laughed. 'This'll be a nice surprise for you, then. Our Edgar is going to be a big brother.'

Hugh stopped and looked hard at me. 'Collette's pregnant?'

'So she says.'

Hugh shook his head and continued walking. 'When's she due?'

'Any day now, apparently.'

'Is she telling the truth, do you think?'

'How the fuck should I know?' I said.

'Well ... have you noticed any weight gain?'

'Christ, Hugh. Have you seen her recently? It just isn't possible to tell. She's not what you'd call slim at the best of times.'

'No, I suppose not.'

We reached a zebra crossing and paused as a car trundled past.

'Why would she lie about it, anyway?' I said, softening my tone. 'What's to be gained by telling me and Edgar a story like that?'

Hugh sighed deeply. 'I need a drink.'

'I could do with one myself.'

'There's a little place not far from here that I sometimes frequent,' Hugh said.

'Gay bar?'

'Ah, you show your innocence, dear boy,' Hugh said as we crossed the street. 'There are actually very few completely gay bars in this city.'

'Really?'

'Really. There are some, however, that have a high percentage of gay regulars, and yes, this is one of those.'

'I take it they serve cocktails, have Abba's greatest hits on the jukebox, and are more tastefully decorated than your average boozer?'

'I'm going to ignore your feeble attempt at humour. Suffice to say, you will be the scruffiest person in the room.'

'Hell, I'm used to that,' I said.

———

Nick Drake was, in fact, playing quietly over the speakers when we went into the lounge, which seemed a pity. I had been hoping for Erasure, or even the Pet Shop Boys. To double my disappointment, Hugh ordered a pint of Beamish stout. I had the same. I didn't see too many people drinking Guinness, and decided it would be unwise to risk it.

'This is genuinely appalling,' Hugh muttered darkly when we were seated.

'You mean Collette being pregnant?' I said. 'Why so?'

'Do you remember me telling you how bad Edgar was when he came to us, back in the early days?'

'Yes. You indicated his was one of the worst cases of neglect you'd ever seen.'

'It was. Still is.'

I took a sip of Beamish. I don't usually drink it, as a rule, but this was very good: light and fruity for porter, but cool and delicious nonetheless. 'You said that he has never spoken to you about his life at home,' I said. 'It is not beyond the realms of possibility that Edgar is somewhere on the autistic spectrum of disorders. Collette may not have been the most attentive of parents, but his emotional distance may well have nothing to do with her. It could be organic.'

Hugh leaned forward, speaking quietly so only I could hear him. 'Do you know how he ended up in care in the first place?'

'His file indicates that the police called social services.'

'They did, but there's more to the story than that.'

'Oh.'

'It's not a pretty tale.'

'These things rarely are.'

Hugh sat back, looking about the bar. He seemed on edge, out of sorts. I waited for him to continue. I wasn't in any hurry, and knew from experience that he had a flare for the dramatic. 'Do you drink whiskey?' he said at last.

'Whenever I can.'

'Why don't I get us some, and then I will tell you all about it.'

'That sounds like a plan.'

'Do you favour any particular brand?'

'Surprise me,' I said.

He came back from the bar with two glasses of Bushmills and a small jug of water.

'The Smiths lived next door to the O'Sullivans,' he began, pouring a small quantity of water into his glass and swirling the contents before taking a sip and nodding appreciatively. 'They are an elderly couple, their own children having moved away a long time ago. Mrs Smith is a sweet, good-natured lady. She used to be a primary-school teacher.'

He seemed more at ease now, the liquor having dissolved whatever barrier had been causing him anguish.

'Well, they'd lived in that neighbourhood their entire married lives. Most of the houses are Victorian, and many are divided into flats now. That was the case with the building Collette and Edgar lived in. They lived on the second floor. From what I can gather a group of Polish workers took up the ground level, and a young couple were on the third. There was one more apartment above them, in the loft, but it was unoccupied.'

'Is there a difference between a flat and an apartment?' I asked.

'What?'

'You know the way some people talk about flats and some people talk about apartments?'

'Yes.'

'Is there a difference?'

'Um ... I think a flat has to be all on one floor, while an apartment can have an upstairs or a downstairs. I'm not sure, though.'

'Mmm. Me neither.'

'Shall I continue?'

'Please.'

'The Smiths had nothing to do with the inhabitants of the flats. They never had cause to, I suppose. They're not snobby, or anything like that. It just worked out that way.'

'I understand.'

'That all changed one afternoon five years ago. The old couple had been out shopping all morning, and had stopped off at a nice restaurant to have some lunch. They knew something was wrong the moment they pulled into the drive.'

'How?'

'The windows in those houses are made up of six individual panes of glass, divided by a wooden frame. You know the kind.'

'Sure.'

'Well, it looked for all the world as if somebody had taken a paintbrush and daubed dark patterns on each little pane of the two large windows of their living room. They couldn't imagine what could have caused such a thing. Mr Smith went in first, very carefully, because they obviously thought they'd been broken into. He used to be in the army, and is still a very fit man for his age.'

'What did they find?'

'The house was in complete disarray. Furniture overturned, wallpaper pulled off the wall, ornaments smashed, half-chewed food walked into the rugs, and more "paint" smeared all over various surfaces: the television screen, pictures, the refrigerator door. It wasn't paint, of course—'

'Faeces?' I interjected.

'Yes. Someone had rubbed shit all over the place. They didn't need to look closely to ascertain the fact. The stench of it was enough. They followed the trail of destruction upstairs and found Edgar asleep in a cupboard. He was six years old, but so small and emaciated they thought he was maybe two or three. He must have looked like a wild thing: he was dressed in a befouled pair of underpants and absolutely nothing else, black with dirt and a mop of matted hair on his head. They left him sleeping and called the police. Unfortunately, though, the boy woke before the cavalry arrived. Needless to say, he became quite agitated to find two people sitting there watching him. Mrs Smith, very foolishly, thought her teaching experience had prepared her for dealing with distressed children, and she tried to comfort him.'

'I take it she was misguided in this assumption?' I said.

'Edgar fastened himself to her throat with his teeth and refused to let go,' Hugh continued. 'Mr Smith later said he hit and pinched the boy, tried to choke him, too, but it made no difference. He hung on like a pitbull terrier, and simply would not release her. When the police came, they could do no better. Mrs Smith was weak with pain and shock by then, and they were worried about her heart. A doctor was called, a sedative was administered, and unconsciousness finally caused Edgar to relinquish his grip. Poor old Mrs Smith needed three stitches and a tetanus shot. But she lived to fight another day, although it was a terrible ordeal.'

'God love her,' I said, shaking my head in sympathy. 'Poor old dear didn't know what she was dealing with.'

'The police now had a half-naked child, seemingly insane, in their care, and no idea at all who he was or where he came from,' Hugh continued, taking a sip of whiskey and chasing it with a gulp of stout. 'Social services were called, and they had the bright idea of taking a Polaroid of this strange creature and going door-to-door with it. It was one of the Poles in the ground floor flat who recognised Edgar. When the social worker called to the O'Sullivans' abode, she received no answer. A reconnaissance of the rear of the building showed where Edgar had gotten out: he had broken a window and climbed down a drainpipe. The child was taken to an emergency-care unit, and the police, armed with a description of the rather distinctive Collette, parked outside the house and waited for her to show.'

'And?'

'They waited for an entire week. By then, they were working under the not unreasonable assumption that the boy had been abandoned. In fact, that was not quite the case. Collette, you see, had gone on holiday to Torremolinos with a boyfriend, and had not wanted the cumbersome presence of her son to interfere with their merrymaking. So she had stocked up the fridge, bought in a load of bread and cereal, locked him in their flat and left him there.'

I blinked. 'For a week?'

'For a fortnight. She'd been gone seven days when he ran out of food and went looking for more elsewhere—that's how he ended up in the Smiths'.'

'And did she have anything to say in her defence?' I asked incredulously.

'She claimed that her parents had done the same thing to her when she was a kid, and it had done her no harm whatsoever. On the contrary, she always found it a pleasant break, or so she said.

She thought Edgar would enjoy the time to himself.'

'You're fucking kidding me,' I said.

'You know her. She lives in some kind of bizarre alternative universe, where everything is always rosy in the garden.'

'And she has never expressed any remorse or understanding of the damage she did to this kid?'

'Never,' Hugh said. 'I know we didn't give Edgar's disclosure of sexual abuse much of a hearing but, if I'm honest, I've always suspected as much. It adds up. Collette O'Sullivan is a spectacularly needy, psychologically damaged single mother. She is not fit to have a child in her care.'

'What can we do?' I asked. My whiskey was gone. My pint was almost finished, too. They both tasted like more.

'I'll write a letter stating my concerns, and send it into the HSE. Will you co-sign it?'

'Of course,' I said. 'But I'm not sure how much it'll help. The story you've just told me happened years ago, and she has been engaged in regular access. I can't imagine social services will want to remove a child unless they have grounds.' I stood up and motioned at our empty glasses. 'Same again?'

'Yeah, why not?' Hugh said. 'This case is wrecking my head, Shane. I mean, do we have to see another child's life ruined?'

'Maybe we can ensure that doesn't happen,' I suggested. 'Even if a family support worker gets assigned a few hours a week, it would be something.'

'Yeah, that might be enough to keep the kid safe,' Hugh agreed.

'Of course, we don't know who the dad is,' I added. 'He could be very responsible.'

'What kind of a man agrees to have sexual intercourse with that deranged little woman?' Hugh said.

Taking it as a rhetorical question, I repaired to the bar.

When I returned, Hugh was chatting to a slim man with close-cropped grey hair, who was wearing an expensive-looking dark pinstriped suit.

'Well, Hughie, who's the bear?' he said as I set down the drinks.

'David, this is a colleague of mine, Shane Dunphy.'

'Ah, so you're the one he's told me about,' the man said.

'All good, I hope,' I said.

'Oh,' David said, putting his arm round Hugh conspiratorially, 'he reckons you can be a bit on the gruff side from time to time, but other than that, and if one is to ignore the fact that you're unremittingly straight, he thinks you're quite adorable.'

'Oh David, don't be such a pain,' Hugh said, flushing.

'Ah, don't sweat it, Hugh,' I said. 'You're not my type, anyway.'

'Of course not,' Hugh said. 'I know that.'

'You're not sensitive enough to my feelings.'

Hugh blanched. 'Whatever do you mean?'

'Well, you never once commented on the fact that I made such an effort with my appearance this evening. I'm genuinely offended.'

Hugh narrowed his eyes and looked me over. 'New shirt?' he ventured tentatively.

'*Ironed* shirt,' I said.

Chapter 28

The People's Park has a small, wooded area in its centre, which somehow manages to give the impression of a genuine forest while being carefully manicured and in the middle of a busy modern city.

I sat on the grass in this small man-made wilderness with Edgar, a book of old photographs of the city, with commentary by a local historian, spread out between us. I had found the book in the eclectic library Ben had assembled in the loft of Dunleavy House, and I immediately knew Edgar would enjoy it.

I watched as he pondered the sepia-toned images solemnly. Every page was pored over carefully, and the words accompanying the photographs read slowly and deliberately.

Through the trees, I could see a group of teenaged girls in green school uniforms—their hair various fluorescent hues, their make-up awkwardly applied, fake tan plastered patchily over spindly legs—as they walked arm in arm along the path towards the east gate. I wondered idly why school boards always seem to feel the need to dress their students in such appalling colours, but then came to the conclusion that this bunch of youngsters had done their respective appearances so much damage with cosmetics, it scarcely mattered.

Edgar found a picture that had been taken in the park in 1917. It had very obviously been posed, and showed two men, standing in the middle of one of the paths. One had a long, well-groomed beard and was very formally dressed, as if he were on his way to the opera. The other seemed to be a workman of some sort: he had a very unkempt moustache, which grew in a bush over his mouth, and his cheeks were blackened by some kind of dirt or oil. I wondered if he might be a chimney sweep or perhaps a tram or railway engineer.

'Where was this taken?' Edgar asked, without looking at me.

'About twenty yards in that direction,' I said.

'The park looks the same,' he observed.

'Yeah. A lot of the landscaping was done around the turn of the century and it hasn't changed much.'

'Who are those men?'

I checked the text. 'It says here that they don't know. They were probably just passing through so the photographer asked them to stop and pose for him.'

'Their clothes are weird,' Edgar said, rubbing his finger across the dirty cheeks of the roughly dressed man as if he could clean them.

'That's how people dressed back then. If they could look at a photo of you, they'd probably say your clothes were strange, too.'

'I wish there was a photo of Oliver Plunkett before they cut his head off,' Edgar said, as if to himself.

'There are paintings—portraits and stuff,' I suggested.

'I've seen them. They probably don't look much like him.'

'Well, they didn't have cameras then—they used drawings instead. They were usually pretty good, I think.'

'I want a photo of him.'

I watched Edgar, sitting cross-legged on the grass, his face almost touching the glossy pages of the book, his whole body focussed on the activity. The force of his attention was almost a tangible thing. If only I could harness it in some positive way. To achieve that, of course, I would have to have a relationship with the boy—and I was a long way from being even close to that.

'How do you feel about your mum's news?' I asked.

'What news?' he retorted.

'About her having a baby.'

He closed the book and looked about him; it was as if he was suddenly waking up from a deep sleep. 'What about it?'

'Well, how does it make you feel? You've never had a brother or sister before, have you?'

He turned to look at me. I held his gaze. After all this time, I could still read nothing in his eyes—they were devoid even of intelligence. Dead eyes.

'Can I have a look at your phone?' he asked suddenly.

'Why?'

After the annihilation of my bag, I was very wary of giving him access to any of my possessions.

'I want to see what games you have.'

'I have Snake and Pairs. That's it.'

'Can I play Snake?'

I took the phone from my pocket. It was a cheap, basic model. I never have a camera or any other gadgets on my mobile phones, as I only ever use them to make calls or send texts. 'If you want me to trust you with my things, you have to earn that trust,' I said. 'So, if I give you this, will you promise me that you won't drop it in a puddle, bury it in the mud or set it on fire?'

Edgar held out his pudgy hand for the phone. 'I promise.'

I got Snake up on the screen for him, and showed him which keys he could use to move the digital reptile.

'You haven't answered my question,' I said when he was playing, as contented as he ever was.

'What question?'

'About your mum.'

'It's a stupid question.'

'Why?'

'Because you know the answer to it already.'

'Do I?'

'Yes.'

'Tell me anyway,' I suggested.

'I don't feel anything about my mother having a baby.'

'That's kind of weird. Being a big brother is a big deal. Most kids would be going crazy with excitement about it.'

'I'm not most kids.'

That's for sure, I thought. 'Your mum seems pleased.'

He shrugged.

'Do you like to see her happy?'

He said nothing, continuing to play the simple game.

'I asked you if you like seeing your mother happy.'

'I'll tell you something I don't like,' he said.

'What?'

'I don't like this conversation.'

'I wouldn't be a very good friend if I didn't at least try to have it with you, Edgar,' I shot back.

'We're not friends, Shane,' he said. 'You see me because they pay you to do it.'

'That's true. But you know what? At least I'm trying. You've done your best to make me hate you, but I'm still here and I haven't stopped making every effort to get through to you. Come on, kiddo, you've got to give me credit for that.'

'I always thought you were just stupid,' Edgar said.

'No, just stubborn.'

'Isn't that a different word for thick?'

'No. In a way, it makes me a little bit like you.'

That stumped him. He said nothing for a while, his eyes on the small screen of the phone.

'Tell me about when you were at home,' I said. 'I don't know anything about you before you were taken into care. You had a life back then. You must have played games and had fun and gone to school. You never talk about it.'

'That's because I don't want to talk about it.'

'Not talking about it doesn't make it go away,' I ventured. 'Everything that happened to you still happened.'

'Talking about it doesn't make it go away, either. It just keeps it floating round in your head and coming into your dreams.'

I tried another tack. 'What's so bad about that? I like thinking about my childhood.'

'Yeah, but you weren't taken into care, were you?'

'That's a fair point,' I said. 'I've worked in places like Bluecloud, though. I have a sense of what they're like.'

'As staff,' Edgar said. 'Not as a kid. You never had to live there. It's different.'

'I suppose it is. I heard the story of how you ended up in care. How you broke into that house. Hurt that old lady.'

'Did you?'

'Yeah. Sounded tough. Must have been very frightening.'

'You'd think, wouldn't you?' Edgar said, deadpan.

I stretched my legs out in front of me on the grass. They were starting to go to sleep.

'Are you saying it wasn't?'

Edgar put the phone down on his lap. 'D'you want to know what was frightening?'

'Yes, I do.'

'Well, I'll tell you, then. Getting put in a new house with a load of kids who looked at me like I was an alien, that was frightening. Having social workers ask me questions I couldn't even understand. Being told I could never go home. Having a queer like Hugh inform me that I was a poor, unfortunate, abused child.'

All this was said in a voice that, for the first time since I had known him, seemed to be teetering on the brink of tears. His eyes remained dry and his posture exactly as it had been, but for a second, I caught a glimpse of the child behind the facade. It was a fleeting thing, but real, nonetheless. I decided to make one last push.

'And weren't you an abused child, Edgar?' I said, not giving him time to think or recover himself. 'Didn't you tell me that yourself?'

He picked up the phone again and resumed playing. 'This is a good game.'

'I'm glad you like it.'

'She used to make me have sex with her. That's what I told you.'

There it was. Just like that.

'Yes, that's what you said.'

'Yeah, well ... it happened. So what?'

'I'm sorry, Edgar,' I said. I wanted to reach out to him, to make him see that I cared, that, even for such a hardened, damaged child, such things were not right. I wanted to, but didn't know how. He was so implacable, so guarded. 'I'm sorry that happened to you.'

'What for? It's not your fault.'

'It's wrong you had that experience.' I didn't want to gush, but I had to make him understand the gravity of what had occurred. This was, for him, almost an academic discussion. He had removed himself so far from the emotion of it that he might have been telling me about someone else. 'It's something children shouldn't have to put up with.'

'I didn't know any different. It wasn't so bad.'

'I don't think that's true.'

He looked over at me. 'At least when she was doing it, she was there. She wasn't around a lot of the time. She'd go out and leave me on my own. Sometimes there was food—sometimes there wasn't. I never knew when she was coming back.'

'Little children shouldn't be left on their own.'

'Nobody can have told her that.'

'Do you really think she didn't know?' I asked him.

'Doesn't matter now. At least she didn't hit me.'

'No?'

'Oh no. She liked to be the nice one. She used to get her boyfriends to beat me if I needed it.'

'No one needs to be beaten.'

'She said I was bad, that I needed to learn. I think I must have been a slow learner, because I'm still pretty bad, aren't I?'

'I think you are very confused and very angry,' I said, honestly. 'I get the sense you want to hurt the world before it gets the chance to hurt you again.'

'Couldn't I just be a mean bad kid?'

'I don't believe there's any such thing,' I said.

'I think you're wrong,' Edgar said.

'We'll have to agree to disagree then, won't we?'

We sat in silence for a while, then Edgar stood up, brushing leaves and grass off himself. 'I want to go home now, please.'

'Okay.'

'You might want to get your phone fixed,' he said, walking away from me towards the path.

I looked at the screen. A page of text was on the display, and all the words were in some kind of foreign hieroglyphics—Japanese or Korean, perhaps. Edgar had gone into the mobile's Settings menu and changed the language. And because I (alas) do not read Asian, I was unable to change it back.

'Edgar, you promised not to damage my phone!' I shouted after him, genuinely annoyed.

'I lied,' he said, and continued walking.

Chapter 29

G regor Blerinca's office was in the basement of his restaurant. There were no windows and the single electric bulb in the lamp on his desk barely illuminated the room, leaving it in a kind of muddy gloom.

When I walked in, Blerinca was seated at a large wooden desk, his hands steepled before him. Standing by the wall behind him was a dark-haired man dressed in a grey suit with an open-necked shirt. He was thin and almost a foot taller than me, with a high forehead and black hair combed straight back. His cheeks were pock-marked and his eyes were so dark as to be almost holes in his pale face.

Years of working with people have made me sensitive to mood, and a palpable atmosphere of malice struck me the moment the office door closed. It was not coming from the old man, who smiled up at me genially, but from his companion, who neither moved nor spoke yet cruelty emanated from him in waves. There was nowhere for me to sit so I remained standing, feeling decidedly uncomfortable. Silence hung in the dark space like dense cobwebs, and from the tall man I sensed the capacity to hurt and befoul and destroy. I had only ever felt such malevolence from a person once before, when I had visited a predatory paedophile in a psychiatric hospital in Dublin as part of a case I was working on. That monster had revelled in the misery he had caused, gleefully recounting the most horrific acts with undisguised pleasure—but I did not sense that from the man I faced in the underground room. No, this person inflicted pain, not out of joy or for pleasure, but because he was good at it. He was a master craftsman, and violence was his métier.

I suddenly realised I was afraid. I pushed the feeling far back into my consciousness and tried to gather myself. Had Blerinca brought me here to kill me? I am not a small man, and have almost always been able to hold my own in physical confrontations. However, looking at the creature who stood in the shadows peering impassively back at me, I knew I would not stand a chance. He would take me apart one piece at a time, and I would be powerless to stop him.

'Thank you for coming, Mr Dunphy,' Blerinca said. 'I must apologise for the spartan nature of my office. When I invite people here for a talk, I do not like them to relax. If you come down here, you are destined to participate in a serious discussion.'

'Well, I am not relaxed, Mr Blerinca,' I said, trying to sound in control. 'I called in to say that I have been permitted to meet your son. I had thought you would be pleased.'

Blerinca's entire visage changed. He said something quietly in Romanian to the thin man, who nodded abruptly and whooshed past me to the door so quickly and silently he was gone before I had even registered his movement.

'Forgive me,' Blerinca said, standing. 'I am used to fighting for what I need and it has become second nature. Come. You will have a glass of wine with me?'

'I'll take some coffee,' I said, relieved at the lightening in mood. 'I was hoping I might see—um, Vladimir, isn't that his name?— this afternoon, and I don't want to be reeking of alcohol when I do.'

Blerinca held the door open for me. 'As you wish.'

'Who is your friend?' I asked as we climbed the stairs to the restaurant.

'Cezar works for me.'

'He doesn't look like a waiter.'

Blerinca laughed with little humour. 'Oh, he is not a waiter. He would not be good at a job like that.'

We sat at a table near the window. Girls in white shirts and short black skirts bustled around us, laying cutlery, hoovering the carpet and preparing for the evening crowd.

'I will meet with your son once to begin with, to assess what, if anything, needs to be done,' I told Blerinca. 'I will report back to you, naturally, but I need you to understand something about my role.'

'Of course,' Blerinca said.

A pretty, sallow-skinned girl brought a tray with two espressos, cream and sugar to our table.

'I do not, and will not, work for you.'

'No?'

'No. I am not here because you asked me to come, or because I am afraid of you, or because you offered to pay me. My focus will be solely on the needs of your boy. I will do what I have to to make his life better. I am, if you like, working for *him*. That means that your wishes are secondary. I am not saying they are unimportant, or that I will not consider them, but they are much lower down my list of priorities than those of Vladimir.'

Blerinca nodded. 'I see. You are very forthright.'

'If I am to work with your family, it is important we are clear on how things must be.'

'I understand.'

I sipped the espresso. It was dense, grainy and very strong, not unlike Greek coffee. 'But do you agree to those terms?'

Blerinca swallowed his coffee in one gulp, like a shot of tequila. 'For now.'

I didn't like the sound of that, but it was too late to go back.

———

Vladimir Blerinca was short, like his father, but slimmer. His hair was peroxide blond and he had used gel to spike it in jagged, asymmetrical clumps. His school uniform had been so altered as to barely be recognisable. I was amazed the teachers permitted it. He had ripped one of the shirt sleeves off at the shoulder; had written the names of various rock bands and slogans across the front and back; a long chain dangled from his left trouser pocket.

He also wore make-up. Not just a little foundation, or Goth-style eyeliner and black nail varnish, but bright red lipstick, mascara, eyeshadow, rouge: it was an all-out feminine application. I stood to greet him.

'Vladimir, this is the man I told you about,' Blerinca said in English. 'I would like you to speak with him.'

I held out my hand, but the boy scowled at me. 'You the head-shrinker?' he asked in an inner city accent that had no trace of Eastern Europe in it.

'No,' I said. 'I'm not a psychologist. Look, what say we go for a walk, and you can tell me whatever you want to say. If you're not into it, or what I tell you doesn't make sense, well, I won't come back.'

I sensed the old man stiffen, but I ignored him.

'For real?' Vladimir said.

'Scout's honour,' I said.

'Okay.'

The boy dumped his schoolbag on the floor, and walked right back out the door. I followed.

———

'So what did he tell you?' Vladimir Blerinca asked as we walked through the early evening crowd.

'That you were unhappy,' I said. 'That he was afraid you weren't right for the kind of life he had envisioned for you.'

'That's for fucking sure,' the boy said, stopping at a shop window full of colourful clothes.

'So what're the problems, then?' I asked.

'What do you think?' Vladimir asked.

'Hell, Vladimir—'

'No one calls me that,' the boy snapped. 'My name is Vinnie.'

'Okay, then,' I said, everything I thought I understood about such things suddenly turned on its head. (Litovoi/Craig; Vinnie/Vladimir—fuck it, I give up!)

'Do you know who I'm named after?' Vinnie continued, his eyes still on the designer T-shirts behind the glass.

'No.'

'Vlad the fucking Impaler. Now that is goddam hilarious.'

I didn't see the joke. 'What's funny about it?'

'I thought you were supposed to be some kind of whizz kid on this stuff,' Vinnie said acerbically. 'You can't see what's right under your nose.'

'Umm ... no. Sorry.'

'I'm *gay*, arsehole. I am a flaming, limp-wristed, shirt-lifting homosexual. I have a huge crush on Colin Farrell, I own every Barbra Streisand movie ever made on DVD, and I listen to musicals from morning till night. They don't come any gayer than me.'

'Oh,' I said, as the penny dropped deafeningly. 'Vlad the Impaler. I get it now.'

———

Vinnie and I sat at a table in a McDonald's on the riverside. I'm not a major supporter of the golden arches, but they do great coffee, and most kids, even older ones, see the chain as some form of magical kingdom. It is almost a comfort zone for a generation bred on round the clock advertising and food devoid of flavour and nutritional content.

'You're sixteen years old,' I said as the boy tucked into a limp-looking burger. 'How can you be sure you're gay?'

'Because I know. Sure, when I was thirteen or fourteen I fluctuated a bit—had a few girlfriends, but I'm nearly seventeen, and I'm perfectly comfortable with this. I am attracted to other guys. Not a little bit, or now and again, but all the time.'

'Are you out of the closet?'

'Yes. Completely.'

'You've told your dad?'

'I have spoken the words at him,' Vinnie said. 'There's a difference. My father does not hear what he doesn't want to. Things that make his life difficult disappear.'

'But that can't happen with you.'

'No. I'm his only son, his heir.'

'And he loves you. Don't underestimate that fact.'

Vinnie snorted. 'Maybe you shouldn't *over*estimate the fact. "Love" is a tired word. My dad likes the idea of having a son, and of loving me in that powerful, masculine, fatherly way. But the reality is a little bit different. I know he's finding me very hard to even *like*, just at the moment.'

'Have you tried to sit down and explain it to him?'

'Now you're being dense again. Men like Gregor Blerinca don't listen to conversations. They give orders. They put plans into operation. They listen to petitions from their minions. I can't remember the last time I had a real conversation with my dad. I probably never have.'

I scratched my beard and looked out the window. A seagull whisked past, riding a thermal.

'And there is absolutely no such thing as a gay Romanian gangster?' I suggested, grasping at straws.

'Of course there is—just not an "out" one. Plenty of buggery goes on behind closed doors, but it's covered up: no one talks about it. Anyway, who says I want to be a gangster?'

'Don't you?'

'No, I fucking don't. I want to be a writer.'

'Yeah? What kind?'

'I'd like to write for the gay press. Ideally, I'd love to work for one of the glossies, but I'd settle for a 'zine to get me started. I just want to write for a living.'

'Good for you. Knowing what you want to do is half the battle.'

'Is it? How the fuck am I ever going to get there? The only thing Dad will agree to my doing in college is business. I can't run away; he'll just send Cezar to bring me back.'

'Yeah, I met Cezar. Scary guy.'

'He's a sick, twisted fuck. And since Petru went AWOL, he's wheedled his way further and further into Dad's good graces. I can't stand him. It's like having a cobra loose about the place.'

I finished my coffee and took out my cigarettes, offering him one, which he took.

'So, where does that leave us?' I asked him.

'You tell me.'

'Well, it strikes me that I need to have a conversation with your father.'

Vinnie shook his head. 'Are you out of your mind? Telling a man in my father's position that his son is gay is a massive insult. He'd be obligated to kill you.'

'Come on,' I said. 'That's stupid.'

'Oh God, I couldn't agree with you more,' Vinnie said. 'But it's the case, anyway. I suggest you go back, tell Dad I'm just as right as rain, and walk away. He'll think you're incompetent, but I'd guess you can live with that.'

'I don't think I can, though,' I said. 'There has to be another way.'

'Shane, he asked you to see me in the hopes you'd cure me. You can't. I'm not ill, or disturbed, or traumatised.'

'I'm not saying you are.'

'He wants me to change, and I'm not going to. In fact, he's the one who should be doing the changing.'

I stubbed out my cigarette and looked at Vinnie. 'I'm going to talk to him, and tell him the truth. We'll just have to see what happens.'

'You're just as macho and ridiculous as he is!'

'No. My job is to help young people. You are now one of my kids. That means we deal with whatever crap comes up. It's what I do.'

'You're a stupid eejit, Shane,' Vinnie said.

'A lot of people have been telling me that lately,' I said.

Chapter 30

M elanie Moorehouse hadn't been to work in three days. No one had seen or spoken to her, and she wasn't answering either her mobile or landline. Her team leader told me where she lived, and I went over after leaving Vinnie.

Melanie's apartment complex was gated. When I dialled her number on the intercom system, to ask her to buzz me in, I got no answer. I tried again, and again. Still no answer. Stubbornness has, in general, stood me in good stead throughout my career, and I saw no reason why it wouldn't come through for me on this occasion. I got back in the Austin and waited.

Twenty minutes later a big, ugly Ford Focus pulled up outside the gate. A hand came out through the driver's side window and waved a card at a small red panel beside the intercom. The gates slowly began to swing open. I switched on the engine, drove up right behind the Ford, and followed it into the complex. The gates closed behind me; I was in.

It took me fifteen minutes of aimless wandering to find Melanie's apartment. It was on the third floor of one of the many blocks, and was up a long flight of stairs. There were no lights on inside that I could see, and repeated ringing of the doorbell elicited no response. I opened the letterbox and peered through. Something inside smelt bad.

'Melanie, I know you're in there,' I lied, loudly. 'Come on, open up. I've come all the way over here to see you, and you don't even have the decency to let me in.'

My voice was met with resounding silence. I didn't let that put me off.

'I think you know that I am an extremely determined sort, and unlikely to be put off by your ignoring me,' I continued. 'So you just keep sitting there in the dark, and I'll stay out here on the landing, bugging you and your neighbours. I might even sing. I've been learning this new song in Scottish dialect. It's called "The Battle of Otterburn", and I've no idea what the words mean, but sure, I need the practice. You can join in on the choruses, if you're up to it.' I started to sing as raucously as I could (the Scots dialect seems to lend itself to enthusiastic, boisterous singing): 'It fell aboot the Lammas-tide, when the muir-men win theer hay. Bowld Douglas boond him a' to ride to England, to drive a prey ...'

I never actually got to the chorus. I heard a shuffling movement, and through the letterbox I saw a bedraggled-looking figure emerge from the doorway to my left, heard the chain being removed from the latch and locks being turned.

'Will you please, please, stop that racket,' Melanie said.

'You didn't like it?'

'Are you coming in or not?'

'Are you inviting me?'

'As long as you promise not to sing.'

I closed the front door behind me, and followed her into what I took to be the living room.

She seemed to have been sleeping on the couch because a crumpled duvet sat atop it. Bottles of what looked like vodka were scattered here and there, and wrappers from bars of chocolate, packets of biscuits and other junk food were lying about. A smell, like blocked drains or open sewage, hung in the air like a bad memory. Melanie had turned the heating up full blast, and that wasn't helping things in the olfactory department.

'So,' I said, moving a pizza box from an armchair. 'What's been up with you?'

Melanie was wearing an old, threadbare dressing gown. Her

hair was awry, but in the darkness I could not see her face.

'Things haven't been so good, Shane,' she said, her voice hoarse and ragged. 'Not good at all, in fact.'

'How so?'

'I tried to kill myself.'

I nodded and took a deep breath. I wanted to go over to her and hold her, but I wasn't sure whether she was drunk or sober, and I had to be careful not to cross any lines of propriety. She was vulnerable now, and it wouldn't do for her to get confused about my role.

'Would you like to tell me about it?'

'There's not much to tell,' she said, and I could hear that she was crying. 'I swallowed a bottle of sleeping pills and washed it down with a bottle of vodka and some cheap rum I had lying around.'

'But you're not dead,' I said—Shane Dunphy, Master of the Obvious!

'No. I think it was the rum that caused my cunning plan to fail. I'd had it in the back of my broom cupboard for a long time, half a bottle of the stuff, as a sort of emergency stash. I didn't think booze could go off, but it looks like it can. I swallowed most of the bottle, and lay down, waiting to pass out. Only I didn't. I fell asleep all right, but a while later I woke again, with a terrible ache in my gut. I shit myself and then puked everything up all over my bedroom.'

'Nice.'

'Yeah. I think you can still get the aroma of that delightful little event. I haven't been able to go back in there, so the room hasn't been cleaned. I've slept in here since.'

I went over and sat beside her. She didn't look at me—her hair was over her face—but I could sense her body shaking from her crying. I tentatively took her hand and squeezed it. 'What's wrong, Mel? Can't you tell me, sweetheart? Whatever it is, we can try and fix it.'

'Some things can't be fixed,' she said, and then the crying overwhelmed her, and she was wracked by sobs that came from deep within, a well of grief that seemed to have no bottom. I held her to me and let her cry until all that came from her were dry rasps and she lay pressed against my shoulder, exhausted.

'There are some things that seem insurmountable,' I said, my voice almost in a whisper. 'But that doesn't mean they are. I can't help you if you don't tell me what's wrong.'

She pushed herself away and sat up; the terrible fit of crying seemed to have brought her back to herself somewhat. 'What do you never say to a child who has just told you they've been abused?' she asked. It was a question you might put to a first-year childcare student: simple; rhetorical, almost.

'You never say: it'll be all right,' I answered, realising as I said it what she was telling me. 'Because no matter what you do, you can never take the abuse away.'

'See,' Melanie said, her head in her hands, her voice muffled. 'You can't help me. No one can make it all right for me again.'

———

While Melanie showered I got a bin liner and cleared away all the bottles and rubbish from the living room. I took another into her bedroom and, holding my breath, bundled the soiled linen into it and tied the bag up to seal away the stench. I opened some windows to let the night air in, and the place didn't seem half as oppressive.

I had a look in her cupboards to see if there was the makings of anything comforting (and easy on the stomach) for her to eat. The options were decidedly limited, but I found a bag of Basmati rice and some stock cubes, and her fridge offered Cheddar cheese, an onion, some herbs and a shrivelled-looking clove of garlic. I found some frozen garden peas at the back of the freezer, which was badly in need of defrosting. I went about making a risotto.

Melanie came out of the bathroom, the rather pitiable robe back round her, and padded into the kitchen.

'Why don't you get dressed?' I asked. 'I've got supper on.'

'What the fuck could you make with what I've got in?'

'A magician never reveals his secrets,' I said, winking. 'Seriously, go and put something fresh on. You'll feel much better.'

'That would mean venturing into my room.'

'I've cleaned up a little in there. It's a bit more hospitable.'

She looked at me, aghast. 'You didn't need to do that,' she said. 'I didn't want—'

'I held my breath and closed my eyes,' I said. 'You can soak the sheets and put them through the wash yourself—but at least it's started, eh?'

She lowered her head, like a shy child. 'Thanks. I suppose I'd better go and beautify myself, then.'

While she was gone I laid the table. I found a bottle of chardonnay in the cupboard with her water glasses, and poured it down the sink. I was certain that a thorough search of the apartment would turn up many similar bottles.

When Melanie came out, I added the peas and herbs to the risotto, seasoned it with salt and black pepper, and finished it with cheese. I would have loved some fresh parsley or tarragon and some wild mushrooms, but none were to be had.

'I hope you don't mind this without cream,' I said, 'because there isn't any.'

'No, it looks very good,' she said. 'Don't give me too much, okay? I'm not sure how I'll cope with it.'

Despite the limited ingredients, the rice was delicious. Melanie wolfed hers down and asked for more, which was heartening. As she polished off the remaining mouthfuls on her plate, I boiled the kettle and made us a pot of coffee.

'It happened in a pub, three weeks ago,' Melanie said as we sat over steaming mugs and smouldering cigarettes. 'I'd gone in for lunch, as you do. I'd been to this place hundreds of times before, and there had never been any problems. But on this particular day, the second I walked in, I thought I was going to pass out.'

'I'm sorry, Mel,' I said. 'I don't understand.'

'They'd changed the fittings—the wood, the furnishings. The new ones were a kind of dark lacquered colour. That was what did it. That awful fucking colour. He'd had it in his place, you see.'

I was still uncertain what she was trying to tell me, but I thought saying nothing might be the best course of action, so I poured myself some more coffee and patted the back of her hand. 'Tell me,' I said.

'I grew up in a little village in the west,' Melanie continued. 'There was only a post office, a pub and the local shop. On our way to and from school, Yasmin, my little sister, and me would have to walk past the local pub. Jamesie, the old guy who owned the place, would sometimes bring us in to have a glass of orange. I say he was old—he was probably in his forties, maybe even younger. Everyone seems old when you're a kid, don't they?'

'Yeah, they do,' I said. I don't think she even heard me.

'It wasn't just Yasmin and me he'd talk to. He was like that with a lot of the kids in the village. We all loved him. He'd have a few sweets to give us, or some toy or other. We'd almost hope he'd be out front, sweeping the fag butts off the pavement, so he'd stop and chat. On my eighth birthday, he started taking us out the back.'

I squeezed her hand. I knew what was coming next, although I hoped against hope that I was wrong.

'It started out with just fondling. He wouldn't really say much, just put his hands on us. Poor little Yasmin—she was only six— she used to just freeze up. I'll never forget the expression on her face. I remember trying to get her to talk about it afterwards but she wouldn't. "He told us we'd die if we ever told," she'd say. I don't think he ever did say that, but it was what she heard.'

'And did you ever tell?'

'Once. It got worse, you see. He started to want to fuck us, and Yasmin was just too little.' She was crying again, tears rolling down her cheeks. I think I might have been, too. She held my hand tightly, and the words tumbled out of her like an avalanche. Now the story had begun, there could be no stopping it. 'I thought he'd kill us, sooner or later. I tried to tell my mum. I said I didn't want to speak to Jamesie any more because he was hurting me. She looked at me, all strange, and asked me what I meant. I didn't have the right words to describe it. The only ones I knew were curse words: fuck and cock and fanny and whatnot. I told her, as best I could, and she slapped me. I was so surprised, I didn't even cry. I just said sorry and went up to my room.'

'Ah, love, I'm so sorry,' I said. 'She should have done something.'

'This was way back. There were no sex-abuse scandals, back then. AIDS hadn't even been heard of in Ireland. This was beyond the realms of her experience. She walked us to and from school after that, though. I'll give her that.'

'But she never called the police.'

'No. In our village, the scandal would have been ferocious. People wouldn't have understood.'

I lit another cigarette from the butt of the old one. 'So you had to live the rest of your childhood only a few yards away from the man who had done those things to you. You had to see him coming and going about his day-to-day business, you had to pass by him with your mother or father and pretend everything was normal.'

'Yes.'

'Probably wondering who else he was doing it to.'

'I'm ashamed to say, Shane, that never crossed my mind. I was just glad he wasn't doing it to me any more.'

'You were a child. You focussed on surviving.'

'When I went into that pub here in the city,' she said, 'everything came rushing back. I'm not saying I repressed it, or forgot about it. I'd just ... I'd just stopped thinking about it. It wasn't something I needed to have in my life, so I'd pushed it aside. And eventually, it was as though it was gone.'

'Only it wasn't.'

'No. When the memory resurfaced, it was like I wasn't me any more. Everything I knew about myself was wrong. I was soiled, damaged. I felt like an open wound, a cut that had never healed.'

'And the alcohol helped to cleanse it,' I said. 'And it anaesthetised you.'

'Yes. But I found that I couldn't really work. Not just because I was hung over. When I came face to face with a parent I knew was neglecting or abusing their child, I wanted to throttle them. When I encountered a hurt kid I wanted to run away from them, screaming, because all I saw was myself. Jesus, Shane, I'm a fucking mess.'

'No. You're in pain, right now. But you've faced up to it. You've spent a lot of years pretending to be someone else, but tonight, here, you're whole. This thing that happened—it's a part of who you are. It doesn't define you, or even alter you, but it is a piece of the whole picture. You just need to rearrange your sense of self round it.'

'Just like that.'

'No—with help. You need some therapy, Mel. Maybe a lot of therapy. And you have to stop drinking.'

'I already have.'

I grinned. 'How many bottles are there hidden around the apartment?'

She sighed and took another cigarette from my pack. 'One or two.'

'They need to go.'

She sighed deeply and leaned her head against me. 'I don't know if I can do it,' she said. 'It's just too hard.'

'You've got a lot of help,' I said. 'More than most people.'

'Why doesn't that make me feel any better?'

'I don't think much will, just at the moment,' I said. 'But you *will* feel normal again. In time.'

And then we didn't say anything else for a while.

Chapter 31

It was six o'clock in the morning before I arrived home. Melanie had fallen asleep on the couch sometime around four. I made up her bed fresh, and carried her to it. She gripped me like a small child, terrified to be left alone, but then drifted back to unconsciousness when I covered her with the duvet and tucked her in. I left a note saying I would tell her team leader she was ill, and I would call the following evening to make sure she was okay.

As I opened my door, I felt exhausted and raw inside. I wanted to fall into bed myself and not wake up until the world seemed a more hospitable place. I sat down heavily on the couch, thinking dolefully that my first meeting of the morning was in three hours' time. It was too late to cancel it, and there seemed little point in going to bed. I was putting on the kettle for coffee when there was a knock on the door.

I couldn't think who would be calling so early. My door doesn't have a safety chain, or one of those peepholes where you can see who is on the other side. I didn't feel inclined to just fling it open, though, so I put my hand on the handle, and called loudly: 'Yeah? Who is it?'

'It is Petru Tomescu,' came the reply. 'Please let me in. I need to speak with you.'

Petru looked awful. He was dressed just as he had been when I had last seen him in the hospital, and he stank of sweat and dirt. His jeans were filthy, and his leather jacket was zipped to the neck, even though it was, if anything, a little too warm in the apartment. His face was very pale, but there were florid, feverish marks on his cheeks, and dark rings under his eyes. He sat down stiffly in one of my armchairs.

'Where have you been?' I asked, in no mood for delicacy. 'Elvira has been out of her mind with worry. I've looked everywhere for you, man!'

He gazed at me with lidded eyes. 'Can I trust you, furniture man?'

'Can we dispense with the furniture man nonsense?' I snapped. 'You knock on my fucking door at the crack of dawn, and then come in here trying to antagonise me. What's wrong with you?'

He sucked in a breath, as if it hurt him to do so. 'I need to know you will do something for me.'

'What?'

'You must carry a message to my wife and son.'

'Tell them yourself.'

'I cannot. It would endanger them.'

I walked out to the kitchen and began to make the coffee. I could hear his raspy breathing from where I stood.

'What message would you like me to pass on?'

'You will do this for me?'

'Tell me the message first.'

'I want them to know that I have accomplished what I set out to do.'

I brought the coffee in to the living room and sat opposite him. 'What the fuck does that mean?'

I tapped out a cigarette and offered him one. He took it gratefully. I tossed my Zippo over, but his hand was shaking too badly and I had to light the smoke for him.

'Elvira will know. She will tell Litovoi when he is old enough to understand.'

'Petru, I'm not from your world, I'll be the first to admit it,' I said, trying to sound reasonable. 'I know you're in some kind of trouble, and your boss tells me you're off on a fucking crusade ... I don't really understand the ins and outs of it all. But the way I see it, there are two options available to you now.'

I poured a cup of coffee and gave it to him.

'And what are these options?' Petru said, a hint of amusement in his voice.

'You could hand yourself over to the police. They would offer you some kind of protection. If you are genuinely under threat if you return to Romania, you'll surely be granted refugee status.'

'And the other option you spoke of?'

'Go to Blerinca. He loves you like a son, Petru. He'll make sure you're kept safe. I know he's been watching over Elvira and Litovoi.'

Petru sipped the coffee and nodded.

'Will you tell my wife the words I said?'

'Yes.'

'Will you mention to anyone else that I was here?'

'No.'

He stood up. It took him two attempts to get out of the chair. 'Thank you for the coffee. May I have another cigarette, please?'

I handed him the pack. 'It's not too late to turn this round,' I said, as I walked him to the door. 'Think about what I said.'

He nodded and was gone. I went back in and watched the early news broadcast and ate some toast. It would soon be time to go to work. As I stood up to get my coat an hour and a half later, I noticed an odd stain on the armchair where Petru had been sitting. I touched the wide spot, which was brownish, almost black, and tacky to the touch. If I wasn't such a down-to-earth type of person, I might have thought that Petru Tomescu had been wounded and had bled all over my seat.

Chapter 32

I had two case review meetings that morning, which I got through on autopilot. At lunchtime I called Melanie. She was feeling better, although naturally embarrassed by what she perceived as such a display of weakness the previous evening. I told her to snap out of it and not be so daft—the shame would have been if she had not asked for help when she did.

At two that afternoon, I was sitting opposite Gregor Blerinca in his grim, tomb-like office. He had ensured there was a chair for me this time, and the bulb in his lamp seemed equipped with a bit more wattage. The old man smiled indulgently at me. I wondered how friendly he would feel after he'd heard what I had to say.

'You have a very bright, strong-willed son, Mr Blerinca,' I said. 'You should be proud.'

'Vladimir is a good boy,' Blerinca agreed. 'Can you help him with his problem?'

'I don't believe Vinnie has a problem,' I said, biting the bullet.

Gregor Blerinca's smile faded rapidly. 'You met him. I was there. You saw how he looks, how he dresses.'

'My dad never much liked the way I dressed or wore my hair. He got used to it, eventually.'

'You should see the magazines he reads. The newspapers he brings into my house. They contain material a young man should not concern himself with.'

I took a deep breath and said what needed to be said. 'Mr Blerinca, Vladimir—Vinnie—is gay. He tells me he is a homosexual, and after having spoken to him about it, I think he is probably right.'

Blerinca stared at me in wide-eyed disbelief. 'How dare you come here and say such things to me—'

'Mr Blerinca, it is possible, although unlikely, that this is simply a phase your son is going through. He may grow out of it. However, I would be doing you a disservice if I didn't advise you to prepare yourself for the fact that Vinnie is committed to what some would call an alternative lifestyle, and that he would like to have a career writing for those magazines and newspapers you mentioned.'

Blerinca's mouth was opening and closing like a goldfish, and he had turned a worrying shade of puce. 'You, sir, are a fraud,' he rasped. 'I turned to you because you told me you try to help children and their families. I offer you friendship and you throw it back in my face. You insult me and my son. You are a very foolish man. I will make you sorry. You will eat your words before I am finished with you.'

'You told me you loved your son,' I said, trying to ignore the threat he had just uttered. 'You came to me and said he was unhappy and that you wanted me to tell you why. Well, here it is: your son is gay. He is unhappy because you will not accept this truth, and because you are trying to coerce him into a life he has never wanted. I did exactly what I said I would. I'm sorry if what I'm telling you isn't what you wanted to hear, but I did warn you that might happen.'

'Your job is to fix things like this!' Blerinca shouted. 'Tell Vladimir such a life is wrong. That it is a sick and perverted thing to lie with another man. This is what you should do. Go and speak with him now.'

I shook my head. 'No. *You* are the one who should speak with Vinnie. Let him tell you about what he wants from life. You might be surprised at how mature and rational he is.'

'I know where you live,' Blerinca hissed. There was nothing of the sweet, grandfatherly old man about him now. His voice dripped with vitriol, and I realised Ben had been right: I had made a terrible mistake. Any other day, I probably would have stood up and walked away, leaving him to rant and rave to the four walls. That afternoon, however, I was aching with tiredness, worried about my friend and generally in a bad mood. The Romanian's last comment made me see red.

'You miserable, self-centred old goat,' I said, my own voice raised now. 'Do you know my boss didn't want me to meet your son? He thought you should be left to wallow in your own misery. I spoke up on your behalf, because I genuinely believed you cared about your boy's welfare. I did *you* a favour. And now, you aggressive, rude little *arse*, you have the gall to threaten me? What kind of uncivilised, medieval thug are you?'

'Be very careful what you say to me. You have already made one mistake today,' Blerinca seethed.

'Well then, another one hardly matters, does it?' I snapped back. 'Let me tell you this: my superiors know that I am working with you. My organisation has a lot of money, and often works with the Gardaí. If anything should happen to me, you will find so many police watching your every move that taking a dump will become a spectator sport. Also, and perhaps you might understand this point a little better, Karl Devereux, whom I know you are familiar with, is a close friend and associate of mine. If I so much as stub my toe over the next while, I will ensure he makes life very uncomfortable for you and your organisation—and I think you know, probably better than I do, just how capable he is of that.' I stood up. 'You have a fine son. He deserves a better father than he has. Instead of wasting your breath threatening me, you should be trying to make up for the time you've lost.'

I walked out, my heart thumping and sweat seeping into the back of my shirt. As soon as I got back to my car I called Devereux and left a message for him to ring me back as soon as possible. Half an hour later, he did.

'What's so urgent?' he asked.

I told him.

'You handled that well,' he said, not even trying to hide the sarcasm in his voice.

'How bad is it?' I asked, dreading the answer.

'Pretty bad. I'll see what I can do.'

'Thanks.'

'Do you have anywhere else you can stay for a night or two?'

'Will I be bringing shit down on someone else?'

'No. Work on the assumption it was an idle threat until I tell you otherwise. Going on a sleepover for a few nights will just put my mind at ease, okay?'

'Okay. And you'll call Blerinca? Try and smooth things out?'

'Consider it done.'

'I should have listened to you, shouldn't I?' I said, gripping the wheel. 'This is way out of my league.'

'Don't worry,' Devereux said. 'He was probably just blowing off steam. I'll talk to him.'

I stopped off at my apartment and picked up an overnight bag, then drove a circuitous route to Melanie's place. I figured she wouldn't mind a house guest for a few nights.

Chapter 33

Collette O'Sullivan had her baby at three o'clock in the morning of my first night sleeping on the couch at Melanie's. Hugh called me at seven to inform me of the news.

'A little girl. Six pounds seven ounces. Collette is calling her Terri.'

'How's Edgar taking it?'

'I haven't told him yet.'

I was surprised at that. 'Why the hell not?'

'He gets up every day, regardless of whether he's in school or not, at eight o'clock. My going in and giving him this information will not alter that one iota.'

'I presume mother and baby are doing well?'

'Positively blooming.'

I sat up on Melanie's couch, which was far from comfortable. I had caught perhaps two hours of rest, and was stiff and irritable from lack of sleep. I looked out the window at the brightening day. 'You planning on bringing Edgar over to see them later today?'

'Probably just before lunchtime. One-ish.'

'Mind if I tag along?'

'Not at all. It'll be nice to have the company.'

'Okay, then. I'll call over at half past twelve, and we can go in the Austin.'

'We'll travel in style.'

'Style is important in this line of work.'

'In *every* line of work.'

'Do we know who the father is yet?' I asked, going into the kitchen and taking a carton of orange juice from the fridge.

'Yes. He's a gentleman of Eastern European extraction. Marius is his first name, I believe. I can't pronounce his surname.'

'Eastern European, eh. There's a lot of it about, these days.'

'I don't follow.'

'Doesn't matter. I'll see you later on.'

'Right you be.'

————

Litovoi was now fully recovered, and had returned to the crèche, where some big changes had happened. Several more children of other nationalities had joined the group, and Irma had made every effort to ensure that the equipment, posters and general ethos were as multicultural as possible. On the morning Litovoi had gone back, he arrived in the playroom to see a large banner hung on the wall, which said: *Întâmpinaphi în spate, Litovoi*— Welcome back, Litovoi. He was delighted when he was told what it said. All the children were encouraged to communicate with one another in the various languages that were spoken in the crèche, and new words were learned every day, which meant that a multilingual vocabulary was being developed by everybody, the staff included.

I sat among the children on one of the low small-world chairs, and listened as Patience, the mother of a Nigerian child, told a story about Anansi, the clever spider. The children all listened, rapt, as Patience, a natural storyteller, if ever there was one, wove a web of magic as beautiful as any Anansi could have created, sharing, with undisguised pleasure, an ancient folk tale from her home.

'One day Anansi the spider picked some very fat and tasty yams from his garden. Yams are a vegetable, children, that we eat in my country, sort of like potatoes, but much sweeter. Anansi was a wonderful cook, and he baked those yams in the oven with much care and they came out smelling quite delicious. He could not wait to sit down and eat them. Just then there was a knock at his door. It was Turtle, who had been travelling all day and was very tired and hungry. "Hello, Anansi," said Turtle. "I have been walking for so long, and I smelled the most delicious yams I've ever smelled. Would you be so kind as to share your meal with me?" Anansi could not refuse, as it is the custom in Nigeria to share your meal with visitors at mealtime. But he was not very happy, for Anansi was a little too greedy and wanted the delicious yams all to himself. So the clever spider thought to himself and came up with a scheme.'

As a child, I had loved the Anansi tales, as well as their American cousins, the Bre'er Rabbit stories, and I became as engrossed in the naughty spider's antics as the children. It was glorious to see them all, regardless of nationality or creed, gazing wide-eyed as Patience recounted the ancient story.

She followed it with songs about food and sharing, and then the children made some props and costumes and acted out the tale under Patience's kindly supervision. I was amazed at how a play which basically involved two characters could be expanded to involve roles for the entire group, but it was: Anansi apparently had some insect friends staying with him (a ladybird, a beetle and a wasp), who were just as mean as he was to Turtle; there was a group of very sardonic frogs waiting down by the river, and some hilarious fishes. It was an exciting, frenetic but entirely pleasurable few hours of learning, activity, but most of all of great fun. I would gladly have remained for the rest of the day, but I had arranged to meet Elvira to talk about her husband's unexpected visit.

'Don't you see what he was telling you?' Elvira asked tearfully when I had finished giving her Petru's message. We were sitting in a café not far from the crèche.

'Sorry, but I don't,' I said. I had neglected to tell her about the blood. His visit alone was enough for her to have to take in.

'He is saying goodbye to me,' she said, weeping openly. 'He cannot stay hidden for ever. He must leave Ireland, now, or go to his death at the hands of his enemies.'

I shook my head. 'This is crazy, Elvira. There has to be something we can do ...'

She buried her face in her hands. I sat there, feeling sick and helpless as she cried for a love taken by forces beyond her control.

———

Edgar's new sister, Terri, was a beautiful baby. I held her and felt that strange sense of protectiveness and awe I always experience around infants. The miracle of birth is, to me, the most amazing thing there is, and it never fails to enthral me. Terri was almost completely bald with huge deep blue eyes. I touched her tiny, perfectly formed feet, placed my index finger in her palm and felt her incredibly strong grip as she instinctively grasped it in her fist. The baby gazed up at me. I knew from the child-development theory I had studied that she could see and focus upon my face from where I was holding her, and I wondered what she was thinking. How could she understand a world so new and strange without the benefit of language or any real frame of reference? I know we've all gone through the process, but nature has conspired so that we have no recollection of it, and the mystery of how such a small, helpless creature can become a fully formed person, with all the potential to climb K2 or discover a cure for cancer or make another new life from its own flesh and blood remains a wonder to any who pause to consider it.

I held Terri in that sterile, neutrally coloured room, and marvelled that this child could stir such powerful feelings in me. When I passed her over to Hugh, I saw much the same emotions play across his face. Yet Edgar showed no interest in touching his sister, and expressed neither joy nor pleasure in meeting her. Birth had taken some of the spring out of Collette's step, and she talked incessantly about the terrible pain and physical strain of giving birth. In fairness, as a man, I am not in any position to criticise her on making a big deal out of the experience, and I sat and listened as sympathetically as I could. When she got to the part where she told me, quite solemnly, that her 'fanny was all bent out of shape', I felt it was time to call a halt to the visit.

In the car on the way back to Bluecloud, I tried to get a sense of Edgar's state of mind.

'So what do you think of Terri?' I asked, watching his facial expression in the rear-view mirror.

'Dunno,' he grunted.

'C'mon, Edgar,' I said. 'It's not like you not to have an opinion. Out with it: what do you make of her?'

The boy shifted uncomfortably in the back. 'She's very small,' he said at last.

'Yeah, it's always amazing to see just how teensy babies are,' Hugh agreed. 'You would have been like that once, Edgar.'

Edgar shook his head. 'No. I wasn't ever like her.'

Hugh threw me a puzzled look. 'What do you mean?' he asked. 'We were all babies starting out.'

'No. I don't think I could have been.'

Hugh laughed, nervously. 'Of course you were. You're not making sense. Why ever do you think you weren't?'

Edgar gazed out the window as buildings and cars scrolled past. 'She can't do anything, can she?'

'Terri?' I asked. 'No. She needs to be fed and changed and looked after. She'll need everything done for her for a while, Edgar.'

'Well, see, I had to be able to look after myself, didn't I?' Edgar said, slowly. 'Collette never really minded me. I had to do it all. So I couldn't have been like that baby.'

In the rear-view mirror he looked, for the first time since I'd known him, truly sad and forlorn. Life had never been kind to this boy. No one had ever loved him, or offered him comfort when he needed it. As a very young child he'd had to fight for the basic elements of survival, and that battle continued even when he no longer needed to struggle. He was an utterly tragic figure, and I had no idea how to get through to him. He was beyond my skills, and I knew it.

'I don't think I want to go on access visits any more,' Edgar said.

That knocked Hugh and me for six.

'How come?' I asked.

'What's the point?' Edgar said, then lay down on the seat and closed his eyes, as if he was falling asleep.

He would say no more on the subject.

Chapter 34 ❧

D
evereux called to Dunleavy House later that evening to
tell me he had spoken to Blerinca, and that the old man
was as calm as he was likely to get about our altercation.
It was unusual for Devereux to make visits so far out of his usual
territory, but he looked as comfortable sitting in my office as he
did anywhere. I have never actually seen him look ill at ease or out
of his depth. I'm not sure he is even capable of such feelings.

'You might as well go back home,' Devereux said, sitting in
Loretta's chair and placing his feet on her desk. 'If they want to get
you, they'll find you wherever you're staying, anyway. You're not
exactly lying low, are you?'

'I have to work, Karl,' I said. 'I'm not going to bring my life to
a halt because some hood has a grudge against me.'

'He could easily bring your life to a dramatic and permanent
halt,' Devereux said, sharply. 'I've spoken to him, however, and he
knows you are under my protection. You're as safe as you can be,
under the circumstances.'

'I'm sorry I dragged you into all this,' I said. 'I know I had no
right to ask you for help. You turned your back on this type of
crap a long time ago.'

Devereux shrugged and put his hands behind his head. 'I don't
think you *can* really put it behind you,' he said. 'It's a part of who
you are—how you think, how you understand the world, how you
interact with people.'

'I understand,' I said, 'but that doesn't mean you want to go
ploughing right into the middle of a gang war.'

'True. But there was a part of me that wanted to get involved.

It was a little bit like taking a friend round my old neighbourhood. I kind of enjoyed it.'

'Really?'

'I know those people, Shane. It's familiar. Like a comfortable pair of slippers. Besides, you have every right to ask for my assistance.'

'Do I?'

He smiled, a kind of pursing of his thin lips. 'Very few social care professionals will even give me the time of day because of who I am—what I am—and where I come from. To them I am an ex-con and an anachronism. You treat me with respect. Where I come from, that commands respect in return. I appreciate it a great deal.'

I blinked. This was as close to bonding as I had ever come with Devereux. I wasn't sure how to respond to it.

'I treat you as a professional because you are one,' I said, tentatively. 'Your history is of no consequence, except that it gives you knowledge I don't have. I respect you because you are good at what you do, and you care about the people you work with. There's a hell of a lot of "professionals"'—I made inverted commas in the air with my fingers—'who seem to see the kids and their families as nothing more than a quaint problem to be solved. For you, they are real people. You understand them. I hope I do, too.'

'From what I've seen, you do.'

'That doesn't take away from the fact that I have put you in a position where you have had to fall back on your previous role as an enforcer or whatever,' I said. 'I don't think that is particularly respectful to you.'

'You didn't do it on purpose,' Devereux said. 'And it would have been stupid of you to sit back and wait for Blerinca to launch an attack. You were right to call me. I'd have been annoyed if you hadn't.'

'And what if Blerinca *does* try to hurt me?'

'I don't believe he will.'

'Why?' I asked, genuinely curious.

'Because he told me he would not.'

'Karl, he's a criminal. Hardly the most trustworthy of individuals.'

'In Blerinca's world there must be trust. What gives him power is that he does what he says he will do. If he says he will kill you, then he will. Conversely, if he says he will not, he will not.'

I nodded. 'Is that how you were?'

'It is how I am.'

We sat in silence for a time. Devereux is one of the few people I know who does not feel the need to fill every lapse in the conversation with chatter. Because he is comfortable with quiet, I find that I am too.

'I think Petru Tomescu is dead,' I said, after a time, and told him of the early morning visit, and Elvira's interpretation of it.

'I'm afraid I must concur,' he said.

I shook my head. 'I don't know how people live like that,' I said. 'I thought we had evolved beyond that as a species, that kind of indiscriminate death. What does it serve? Who gains from that kind of violence?'

'Many people. And there is a never-ending supply of young men all too willing to put themselves in the line of fire—to prove themselves, to earn money, to gain respect and credibility—and as long as those men are there, the war will never end. Someone, somewhere, will always be engaged in it.'

'You paint a grim picture,' I said.

'Grim, but real.'

'Not my reality.'

'It is, partly,' Devereux said. 'You skirt the periphery of it. Your name and face are known by those who live in that world. Every now and then you stray over the line because your work requires it. Every time you do, you become that little bit more aware of what goes on in the shadows. The shapes become clearer to you, and you to them. That's the way it works.'

'Perhaps,' I said. 'It doesn't mean I have to like it. And I won't let it take me over.'

'Honourable,' Devereux said. 'I hope the day won't come when you don't have a choice.'

Chapter 35 ∾

Even though I had only really been away from home for one day, it felt like longer, probably because I hadn't actually slept in my own bed for two nights. I was glad to stretch out in my room that evening at ten-thirty.

I remember a muddled dream, where I was on a stage in front of everyone I knew, trying to play a tune on an ancient Stroh violin. Every time I touched one of the strings with the bow, it made a sound like a baby wailing, and the audience would all put their hands over their ears and boo me. I saw Ben Tyrrell, his face twisted in an expression of dismay; Melanie, a bottle of Bacardi in one hand, shouting up at me to get off the stage; Edgar, doubled over with laughter, Terri held unsteadily in the crook of his arm. I tried desperately again and again to get a note from the instrument, but the cries seemed to become more and more urgent, and as they reached an almost deafening cacophony, I shot up in bed, drenched in sweat and wide awake.

I knew immediately that something wasn't right. I had the distinct impression that something other than the nightmare had disturbed my sleep. I sat very still and listened.

I am not a squeamish person, and have never been afraid of the dark even as a child. I strained my ears for several moments, waiting for whatever it was to repeat itself, but nothing came. Traffic sounds drifted up from the street, and the muffled noise of a television came from the apartment above mine. Other than that, all was quiet.

I lay down again and tried to go back to sleep, but a nagging anxiety caused me to toss and turn. I went into the bathroom and splashed water on my face; I'd seen people do it in films, and it always seemed to help them. It simply left me with a wet face. I looked at the clock on my phone. It was a quarter past two. Finally, to put my mind at ease, I pulled on a pair of shorts and a T-shirt, and went to check the living room and kitchen.

It's funny how the eye can sometimes refuse to register what it sees. When I went back to my bedroom and opened the door, instead of being faced with the wall opposite it, all I could make out was blackness. I blinked and shook my head, and the darkness morphed into a shape: a man—tall, thin, and motionless. I closed my eyes tight again, and took a step back, but a sinuous arm reached out and grabbed my shoulder.

I recall that I felt no fear. I was still at the point where it all seemed too unreal to actually be happening. I twisted backwards and to the left, trying to escape my assailant's grip, and brought my fist down on the arm as hard as I could. It was like hitting stone, and suddenly the world tipped dizzily at a 180-degree angle. I landed with a thud on my side, wondering how I had gotten there, and then something struck me hard in the larynx, and I couldn't breathe.

That was when I started to get frightened.

———

I must have blacked out, or at least my conscious mind had shut down for a minute or so, because the next thing I remember is sitting in my living room in the same armchair Petru Tomescu had slumped in when he came to see me. Gregor Blerinca was standing over me, and beside him the man he had called Cezar. Blerinca was dressed in a dark brown suit, with an open-necked white shirt. Cezar was all in grey: a tight polo neck, slacks, plain shoes and a long overcoat. The overhead light had been switched on, and it was the first time I had seen Cezar out of the shadows.

There was something reptilian about him. His hair was sleek and seemed to be all one piece rather than millions of individual follicles. His skin shone, as if it had been polished, and his eyes were narrow, slitted and very cold. He was impossibly pale, as if he never saw the sun, and he stood with his feet slightly apart— balanced—ready to move in an instant. I looked up at him, and then away again. He was not outwardly ugly, but there was about him such a sense of peril that I found him repulsive.

'Why have you broken into my home?' I croaked to Blerinca. It hurt to speak. I rubbed my throat where Cezar had kicked me.

'Come now, Mr Dunphy,' the older man said. 'Surely you know why I am here.'

I cleared my throat. I thought I could taste blood in my mouth. 'Are you angry with me?' I asked, knowing it was a ridiculous question, but trying to buy some time, to keep him talking.

'Now why should I be angry?' Blerinca's voice was warm, fatherly, almost.

'Because I told you the truth,' I said.

'What truth did you tell me?'

'I told you that your son was unhappy. I told you what he feels—what he is.'

'And what is my son, Mr Dunphy?' Some of the warmth seeped away. I was in dangerous territory, now.

I looked at Cezar again. His hands were behind his back, and he was a good four feet away from me, but I knew he could cover the distance before I could even be halfway to standing. I swallowed and tried to think of an answer that would not end in further violence. Blerinca snorted in derision.

'Are you afraid of Cezar, Mr Dunphy?'

'I would be foolish not to be.'

'You are honest about that, at any rate,' Blerinca said. He sat down on the couch and looked at me solemnly. 'Your friend, Mr Devereux, called me, you know. He asked me to forget about the words that were spoken between us. He told me you were like family, and that a move against you was a move against him. Do you understand what that means, Mr Dunphy, the commitment Mr Devereux has made for you?'

'I think so.'

'You think so?' The words were heavy with sarcasm. 'Well, let me explain it, so we can be certain you are not confused. It means that if I have Cezar kill you, Mr Devereux will be obligated to kill him. Now, wouldn't that be an interesting competition? Do you think your friend could best mine?'

The situation seemed to be getting more surreal by the second. Even though I was purposefully not looking at him, I could feel the threat exuding from Cezar. It hummed in the room like electricity.

'I never asked him to do that,' I said. 'I would not ask Karl to risk his life ...'

Blerinca nodded. 'I see. But you did ask him to speak with me.'

'Yes but—'

'What did you think he would say? How did you envision that conversation progressing?'

'I didn't—'

'No, you didn't think, did you?' the old man snapped. 'You thought you could play around in my life and that of my family and then just walk away, feeling smug and superior. I'm afraid that some things are not so simple.'

The conversation was getting away from me, and I knew it. But I was beginning to get annoyed. I had never agreed to play the game by Blerinca's rules: I was not a criminal. I was simply trying to do my job, honestly and without compromise. What right did Blerinca have to invade my home like this? This was my place, a space I had made, imprinted with my identity: some furniture; musical instruments; CDs, records and tapes; probably more books than I needed; mismatched, unfashionable clothes— nothing to anyone else, hugely important to me. I had not said these men could come here. And anyway, I had only met Vinnie at

Gregor Blerinca's request.

The words were out of my mouth before I realised it: 'You asked me to help you! You came to *me*, for God's sake—'

I knew as the exclamation came tumbling out that I had let the genie out of the bottle, and that his wrath would be terrible. I saw Cezar move, but it was as though someone had hit a button and everything was happening in slow motion, yet still far too quickly for me to keep up. Suddenly, the terrible man was right beside me, his face millimetres from mine, his hot breath, which, peculiarly, smelt of cinnamon, blasting into my cheek. My groin exploded in agony, and I realised he had gripped me there and was crushing my testicles. I roared full-throatedly and thrashed from side to side, but his grip was immoveable. Tears streamed down my face and in that moment of blind panic I did the only thing I could think of. In fact, I'm not even sure thought had anything to do with it. Blinded by pain, a bitter, ferocious anger building up in me at the wretched unfairness of it all, I pulled my head back and smashed it into Cezar's nose.

I felt his grip release, and then I was pushing myself backwards with as much strength as I could muster. Awkwardly, I slid over the arm of the chair and landed in a heap on the floor. I tried to stand, but couldn't. My legs buckled, and my balls felt as if they must surely explode with pain. Dizziness and nausea crashed over me and I threw up on the carpet. Through my misery I could hear Cezar panting and muttering something. His voice was rasping, other-worldly. I sensed movement behind me, and rolled over. My vision swam, and I was momentarily crippled, but anger was driving me onwards. There was no going back now.

'Come on, you fucker,' I shouted, and the words seemed to be coming from someone else. I felt outside of myself, far away. 'You can kill me, but I'll fucking take lumps out of you before you do it.' Shadow and light played across my vision, and something gripped me by the hair, yanking my head back. I gritted my teeth and lashed out with my fists.

'*Enough!*' Blerinca roared.

Words were exchanged in Romanian, and I was released. I slumped back on to the floor, dazed and ill.

I came back to myself slowly. Looking up, I saw Cezar leaning against the door jamb, a blood-soaked handkerchief pressed to his nose, which was swollen and misshapen. Blerinca spoke to him quietly. The thin man nodded, straightened up, and walked out. His boss turned and gazed at me, tenderly almost, then walked over and extended his hand. I took it and he pulled me up so I could sit on the chair again.

'Do not fool yourself that you are some kind of champion,' Blerinca said when he had seated himself on the arm beside me. 'That was a lucky blow you landed, and Cezar would not have allowed you another. He would have ripped your throat out if I had not stopped him.'

'Why *did* you stop him?'

Blerinca laughed. 'Believe it or not, I did not come here to kill you.'

I laughed at that. 'You're right, I don't believe you.'

'I do not begrudge you your anger,' Blerinca said. 'You have been wronged. I have—how would you say it?—I have *house-trained* Cezar, but he is still very wild. Every now and then I am reminded of just how unpredictable he can be. I did not mean for you to get hurt. Not badly, anyway.'

I shifted painfully. 'If you're not going to kill me, and you don't plan to rough me up any more,' I said, 'would you kindly fuck off so that I can take some painkillers and crawl back into bed?'

Blerinca nodded and stood up. 'I understand.' He walked towards the door.

'Before you leave,' I said as he reached it. 'Why did you come here? And tell me the truth.'

'Two reasons,' the old man said. 'Firstly, to tell you that I accept my son is gay, and that I will gladly take whatever assistance you can offer.'

I shook my head. 'You broke into my apartment in the middle

of the night with a psychotic thug to tell me that? Are you out of your fucking mind?'

Blerinca sighed. 'You disrespected me, the last time we spoke. I have not lived as long as I have by letting such things pass without remark.'

'I'm a childcare worker,' I said, 'not a member of a rival gang. I mean, Jesus Christ, what were you thinking?'

'Can you help me?' he asked. 'I do not understand what Vladimir is going through. I want to be a good father to him, but his is not my world.'

'What was the second thing?'

'I know where Petru Tomescu is.'

That stopped me in my tracks. 'Is he alive?'

'Yes. He was hurt when he came to me, but I had one of my doctors look at him. He is safe.'

'Can you tell me where?'

'Can you help me with Vladimir?'

'How am I supposed to feel safe dealing with you?' I asked, feeling annoyed all over again. 'Give me one good reason why I shouldn't call the police the moment you're out of here?'

Blerinca looked at his shoes. 'I have no reason. I regret what happened. Cezar will be disciplined, I swear it.'

'I'll tell you what,' I said, too disgusted to even look at him any more. 'Just go. Get out of my home.'

He left without another word. I heard the front door clicking closed, and dragged myself upright. Painfully, I made my way out to the hallway, and made sure the apartment was locked and secured. When that was done, I started to shake. I couldn't stop trembling, and slid down the door and sat on the floor. I put my arms around my knees and cried, sobs wracking me until there were no tears left, but still I couldn't stop. Finally I curled up in a ball, my back still jammed against the front door so I would know if anyone tried to come in again, and slept there until the sun came up.

Chapter 36

I was woken by my phone ringing. Woken is perhaps the wrong word, as I had not really slept—my mind had drifted into a kind of neutral place, a sort of stillness. Reality had become too horrific, so I had shut down. The phone rang again. It was in the living room, and I was still in a heap in the hallway, so I decided to ignore it. I heard the rings tapering off as the call went to my message minder. I closed my eyes again. Every part of me hurt, and my stomach was sick and acidic. I just wanted to be left alone. I'd had enough. My plan, such as it was, was to barricade myself into my apartment and stay there for the foreseeable future. I was weary of other people's problems, of the needs and ulterior motives of people I barely knew. I was all used up. The world would just have to get on without me.

The phone rang intermittently for the next hour or so. Then it stopped for a time, and my mind wandered again. Later, I don't know how long, I was roused by somebody knocking on my door. I ignored it.

'Shane?'

The voice was familiar, but I couldn't place it at first.

'Shane, what's wrong? Are you hurt?'

It was Melanie, copying my trick and shouting through my letterbox. I got tentatively to my knees and then stood up. My groin was not as painful as I had expected. I let her in.

'What the fuck happened? Everyone's been trying to reach you.'

'I'm pulling a sickie today, Mel. Maybe for a while, in fact.'

'Why? What's going on?'

I walked stiffly down the hall towards the kitchen. I knew I was dehydrated, but the thought of drinking even so much as a glass of water made my guts heave. Melanie sat at the kitchen table while I told her about my late-night visitation.

'You have to call the police,' she said. 'My God, you could have been killed!'

'I would, except I have my suspicions that Cezar will be long gone. Blerinca didn't actually do anything, other than break in, and he didn't rob me. He'd get a reprimand.'

'Will they come back, do you think?'

'I don't know. I doubt it. If Blerinca had wanted me dead, I'd be dead. If he wanted to scare me, he succeeded. I'm fucking terrified.'

'Are you ... um ... badly hurt? Down there?' Melanie asked gingerly. 'Do you need me to bring you to the hospital?'

'I don't know. I'm sore. I suppose I should get checked out. Why are you here, anyway, and why has the world and its mother been looking for me?'

'Oh, yeah, I forgot. Collette O'Sullivan has done a legger with the baby.'

'How do you mean?'

'Apparently, she walked out the front door of the hospital during the night. She's gone, and so's the little thing.'

I tried to tell myself I didn't care. I rubbed my eyes with the heels of my hands and felt the ache in the pit of my stomach. This was not my problem. Let someone else deal with it.

But Terri is a baby, a voice inside said. She can hardly fend for herself, can she?

'Is she in her house?' I asked.

'No. We've checked. It's empty.'

'What about the father—what do you call him—Marius? Is Collette with him?'

Melanie shrugged. 'No one seems to know where he lives. He's homeless, a lot of the time. Sleeps some nights at the shelter on Vermouth Street.'

'Has anyone spoken to the staff there?'

'I was on my way to do just that, as it happens, when I thought I'd call in on you.'

I stood up. 'Let me throw some clothes on, and we'll go over.'

'No. I'm taking you to the hospital.'

'Let's find Collette and the baby first, eh? Terri's too little to be sleeping rough. It'd fucking kill her.'

'Straight to the hospital after that, though, okay?'

'Deal.'

———

'They were here last night,' Geoffrey, the worker at the shelter, told us. He was the skinniest person I'd ever seen, with an Adam's apple that seemed to bob up and down precariously in his throat as he talked. 'But it was late, and we didn't have any beds.'

'Did they have a baby with them?' I asked.

'A baby? I didn't see one, but they had a bundle of stuff. It wouldn't have made a difference. We didn't have space, anyway.'

'Where would they go when they knew you were full?' Melanie asked.

Geoffrey scratched the back of his head. He had a thick mop of unruly, greasy black hair, and his jaw, which was prominent, was covered in thick, prickly stubble. 'There's a squat Marius has used in the past. It's up in the mountains, an old manor house. A lot of our residents go there from time to time. It's pretty derelict, from what I've seen, but it keeps the weather off.'

'Could you give us directions?' I asked.

'Come on into the office,' Geoffrey said. 'I'll write them out for you.'

———

Melanie insisted that we go to the hospital after we'd been to the shelter, and we spent six hours sitting in casualty before a junior doctor who looked thirteen years old spent three minutes examining me, and then gave me some painkillers. I showed him the tablets I had in my pocket, which I had bought over the counter in a supermarket, and asked him if they were stronger than the ones he had just given me.

'Probably about the same,' he admitted.

'Well, I think I'll stick with my own, then, eh?' I said. 'Is there any permanent damage done?'

'You'll live to fight another day,' he said. 'I wouldn't go climbing any mountains for a week or two, though.'

'Thank you,' I said, and limped out to pay at reception. As I handed over sixty euro, I wasn't sure whether I'd just been ripped off or not.

———

Melanie was waiting in the car when I went outside. Sitting beside her, I lit a cigarette. I suddenly realised that I was utterly exhausted. I hadn't slept properly in days, and was still in shock from my run-in with Cezar. It was four-thirty in the afternoon, and food hadn't passed my lips since the previous morning. I sat back in the seat and closed my eyes. If I was honest, I wasn't sure how much longer I could keep going.

'So you've got a clean bill of health?' Melanie asked.

I faked a smile. 'I'll live.'

'Let's go, then.'

I tried to focus on the task ahead. It was something tangible, something achievable. I was good at my job—I knew that. If I could just keep my mind rooted on doing that, I'd be okay.

'What do we do if we find them?' Melanie asked as she pulled out of the hospital grounds.

'Make sure the baby is all right, and try to persuade them to go back to Collette's house,' I said. 'But if they don't want to, there isn't a whole lot we can do. There's no law against living in a squat.'

'What if it's not fit to have a baby in?'

'We ask them to go back to Collette's, and if they won't, we go and get us an emergency care order and take the baby off them until they see reason.'

'That's a plan, I think,' Melanie said.

'Glad you like it.'

As evening fell over the city, we headed for the hills, and an appointment with a pit full of flies.

Chapter 37

I wrapped myself round Melanie, and tried to shield her from the swarming insects. Above the furious buzzing I could still hear the baby crying. It seemed to be coming from upstairs, but I knew that wasn't possible—the house had no stairs.

Melanie's screaming had become muffled, and I realised the flies were in her mouth—I heard her spitting and retching. I had taken a deep breath at the last minute and was holding it. With my eyes tight closed and my chin tucked into my chest, I shoved us both towards the door. For a moment, I couldn't find the handle, but then I had it and with a lurch we were sprawling on the filthy floor in the hallway. I lunged at the door again to close it, feeling a painful wrench in my groin as I moved too quickly. I could feel the insects crawling on me, but I mashed my fists into my eyes to clear them, then ran to Melanie. She was hysterical, and I grabbed her and began to brush the black crawling things off.

'My hair! They're in my hair,' she gulped after a minute or so. Together we brushed as many out as we could.

When she had calmed slightly, I stood up and repeated the process on myself. The crying had stopped. I wondered if I had imagined it.

'Mel, did you hear a baby just now?'

'What?'

'Did you hear a baby crying?'

'No. I—'

A piercing wail from what seemed to be directly above us cut her off.

'Jesus ...' she muttered.

I stood up and looked at the landing. I couldn't see any way of getting up there.

'Hello!' I shouted up. 'Collette? Are you up there? It's Shane—I only want to talk to you.'

There was no response except an even more urgent bawl.

'They're not here,' Melanie said, her voice very small and quiet. 'They've left her.'

'It looks like it,' I said, and looked desperately about for some way of getting up to Terri. Suddenly an idea occurred to me, and I went as quickly as I could outside and round the rear of the house.

It was as overgrown and wild as the front, but there, leaning against the wall, was a rickety-looking wooden ladder.

'Are you fit to climb that?' Melanie asked behind me.

'I'd better be,' I said. 'Hold the base of it for me, will you?'

I went up as quickly as I could, the cries of the baby urging me onward. The ladder was leaning against the sill of a window that was really just an open hole in the wall: all the fittings—even the frame—had been removed. I climbed in, and found myself in a bare, dust-choked room. Terri was crying enthusiastically now, and I followed the sound. I found her in the corner of a small room to the front of the house, lying in a pile of dirty blankets. There was a bag with cheap nappies and a tin of formula beside her, but no bottles or water. Other than that, I could see no sign that Collette was planning to return. I scooped up the child and shushed her as I walked to the window.

'Got her. I'm going to change her nappy, and then I'll be down.'

Terri's nappy was sodden. She must have been alone for hours. I used one of the clean ones to wipe her, as I had nothing else, and when she was freshly changed, I picked her and the bag up and went back to the ladder.

———

We stopped at a supermarket and bought some baby paraphernalia.

'This stuff is ridiculously expensive,' Melanie observed.

'Just buy it and let's get moving,' I said. Terri had not stopped crying, and I figured, not unreasonably, that she was starving.

As Melanie drove, I held the squalling infant and rang Bluecloud.

'You're bringing her here?' Hugh barked down the phone.

'Where the fuck else am I supposed to take her?'

'We're not equipped to take a baby!'

'Don't worry. Mel and me have been shopping. We've got all the stuff.'

'What,' Hugh spluttered, 'like a cot, and a pram, and a steriliser, and around five hundred changes of clothes!'

'Hugh ...'

'Yes?'

'Shut the fuck up. We'll be there in ten minutes. Have a pot of water boiling. We need to make a bottle up very quickly, and that's as close to a steriliser as we have, okay?'

'All right, but I want it noted that I am not a happy bunny!'

I hung up.

'Is she going to bawl for ever?' Melanie asked.

———

As it happened, once she had downed an eight-ounce bottle, Terri settled quite nicely. Edgar stood in the doorway, watching us very suspiciously.

'Why's she in my house?' he asked.

I had the baby, who was sleeping soundly now, lying on my chest. I was sprawled on the couch in the television room, where Edgar and I had had our first conversation. If he hadn't spoken, I would have fallen asleep myself.

'Your mum and Marius left her alone,' I said, too tired to make up a trite lie.

'I don't want her here,' Edgar said.

'Why not?'

He blinked and seemed to think hard about the answer.

'She makes me feel funny.'

'What kind of funny?'

'Like I want to start crying,' Edgar said, and to my complete amazement, a tear ran from the corner of his left eye. His voice remained the same, and he did not move, but another tear followed the first.

'Crying isn't always bad, Edgar,' I said. 'Sometimes, it's just what we need.'

'I don't like it,' he said, and was gone.

I would have gone after him if sleep hadn't caught up with me.

Chapter 38

'Shane, wake up.'

My hands went to the baby immediately. She was still there, and I relaxed for a moment. I realised that someone had put a blanket over both of us—Hugh, probably.

Ben was sitting on the couch beside me, and Melanie was beside him.

'I've found a temporary foster family for the little one,' he said gently. 'They can take her tonight.'

Tears sprang unbidden to my eyes. Somehow, the baby had anchored me, kept all the dangerous emotions from catching up with me.

'I thought she could stay here,' I said. 'Edgar's here. He's her brother.'

'None of the staff has any experience with babies,' Ben said, his hand on my shoulder. 'This is for the best, Shane. Come on, let me take her.'

I shook my head. 'No.'

Ben raised an eyebrow. 'Do you need a moment?'

'Yes, he does,' Melanie said. 'You go and pack all the baby things into the car. I'll bring her out to you in a few minutes.'

Ben nodded and did as he was told. Melanie looked at me for a moment, then put her arms round me. I held her and Terri and sobbed as though I was a baby myself.

———

I stayed in the TV room while Melanie took the child out to Ben. Hugh brought me some tea and left me. I switched on the box. An old episode of *Star Trek* was playing. James Tiberius Kirk was on a desert planet, fighting a Gorn—something that looked like Godzilla in a multi-coloured leotard. I'd seen the episode before, but I needed something mindless to distract me from just how utterly awful I was feeling, so I sipped the weak tea and watched as the finest captain of the USS *Enterprise* pitted his wits and brawn against overwhelming odds.

'Here's to you, James T,' I said, toasting him with my mug. 'I know how you feel.'

It wasn't looking good for William Shatner when Hugh stuck his head in.

'You okay?'

'Yeah, I'm fine, Hugh. Sorry about earlier.'

'That's quite all right, old man. Listen, I think there's something you should hear.'

'What?'

'Come with me.'

It took me a moment to realise that he had brought me to the door of Edgar's room.

'I was doing the usual rounds of the kids' rooms when I heard him talking,' he said. 'Listen.'

I put my ear to the door, and could hear a voice from inside.

'Who's he speaking to?' I whispered.

'That gruesome picture he has on the wall,' Hugh hissed back. 'He talks to it all the time. Do you think it's healthy for him to do that?'

'Shush a minute,' I said.

'They've taken her away,' Edgar was saying. 'My little sister. That's what she was, Oliver. She was my sister. I've never had a sister before.'

He paused, as if someone was responding to that statement.

'I don't know. See, I don't really behave well with people. I'm mean. I know nobody likes me. And that's all right. I don't mind. But I would have liked her to like me. I told Shane I didn't want her, but that was a lie. I would have been nice to her.'

Another pause.

'Terri her name is. That's a nice name for a baby, isn't it, Oliver? I would have played with her and taught her how to sing songs. I wouldn't have minded if she didn't like Elvis. I would have let her sing whatever songs she wanted. But she's gone now. I probably won't see her again.'

Pause.

'Collette's gone, too. She'll be back, but they won't let her have Terri again. She doesn't know how to mind children, Collette doesn't. Terri's better off with some family that want her. It's just,' and I could hear the tears in his voice, 'I would have liked to be part of her family.'

I pulled myself away from the door.

'Yeah, Hugh,' I said. 'That's probably the healthiest Edgar has ever been.'

I went to the office, and phoned for a taxi to bring me home.

Chapter 39

P etru Tomescu looked thin and anaemic. He had a full beard, now, and was dressed in a shiny, polyester shell suit which was three sizes too big for him. Litovoi was sitting on his knee, hugging him tightly. I could tell from the man's face that this was hurting him quite considerably, but he wasn't about to tell his son that. Elvira was beaming from ear to ear, tears on her cheeks, but pleasure sparkling in her eyes.

'Your debts have been paid in full,' Gregor Blerinca said. We were all in the tiny flat, which had been redecorated and had quite a lot of new furniture besides the sofabed. 'I have seen to it. No one will be looking for money from you ever again.'

'Thank you, Papa,' Petru said. 'I do not deserve this kindness.'

'That is for me to decide,' Blerinca said. 'Now, I must speak to my friend here,' he gestured at me, 'about a personal matter.'

Petru nodded, and Blerinca and I stepped outside.

'Thank you for coming here today. I know you had some concerns about it,' Blerinca said. I leaned against the wall and lit a cigarette.

'I wanted to see that family put back together again,' I said, blowing smoke out the corner of my mouth. 'That's a decent thing you did, clearing their debts. They can actually start to live, now.'

'I wanted to help them,' Blerinca said. 'I am an old man. When I look back over my life, I see I was responsible for a lot of pain. It is nice to be able to identify something good I have done.'

'I imagine it must be,' I agreed.

'Vladimir barely looks at me,' he said, his hands deep in the pockets of his heavy overcoat. 'My own son cannot bear to be near me.'

'He's very angry,' I said. 'He feels you don't listen to him, that you have decided how his life is to be. His vision of it is very different.'

'I know. I have considered that a lot since I last saw you,' Blerinca said. 'I think that Petru could run my business. He would protect Vladimir if he had to.'

'Have you asked Petru what he thinks of that idea?'

'No.'

'You need to start talking to people, Gregor,' I said. 'You accused me once of ploughing around in people's lives—that's just what you do. Petru has been through an awful experience. He might not want to continue in this line of work.'

'He doesn't know any other life.'

'Maybe it's time you both started learning one.'

We were silent for a few moments.

'How can I help my son get what he wants?'

Blerinca looked tired and frail. There was no threat in him now. I almost felt sorry for him—almost.

'Let him apply to do journalism in college. Even if being gay is only a phase, he still wants to write. Let him explore that.'

'Yes, I will.'

'Ask him about his plans and his dreams. Listen when he tells you and don't judge him. Of course there will be aspects of the gay lifestyle that make you feel uncomfortable—parts of it make me uncomfortable—but let that go. It's not a battle you can win.'

'I know that now.'

'If he wants to get some experience on the ground in a newspaper, I know some people I can put him in touch with. He'll just be sweeping up and making tea, but he'll get to see what the work is like. I think that's important. Vinnie probably has ideas about journalism that are based on movies and TV shows. The reality, as I understand it, is a little different.'

'You would do that for us?'

'I would do it for your son.'

'Thank you.'

I flicked the cigarette away and began to walk towards my car. 'Tell Elvira I'll drop by tomorrow.'

'Mr Dunphy,' Blerinca called after me, 'I had a visit from the police yesterday.'

I stopped and turned back to him.

'I called them,' I said. 'I thought about it, and decided that I had to. I told them about your visit to my apartment.'

'Indeed. They were looking for Cezar.'

'He assaulted me. I have to follow the rules of my world, Gregor, just as you must yours.'

'I understand. I also received a visit, a little later, from Karl Devereux.'

'I didn't call him.'

'He was looking for Cezar, too.'

My throat seemed to have gone dry, all of a sudden. I had not called Devereux. I had no desire for him to know what had happened.

'What did you say?'

'I told him what I told the police: that I do not know where Cezar is. It is the truth.'

'And what was Karl's response?'

'He did not say anything. I do not know if he believed me. He is a difficult man to read.'

I nodded and went to my car. I hoped Devereux would not look for Cezar. As I drove away, I prayed fervently that monster would never be heard from again.

Chapter 40

E dgar sat in the pew beside me and looked at the desiccated head of St Oliver Plunkett.

'Terri's new family is really nice,' I told him. 'They're a young couple, and they've fostered babies lots of times.'

'That's good,' Edgar said. He was staring fixedly at the head in its glass case.

'At the moment you can see her on Sundays, for an hour. I know that's not much, and I'm trying to organise a bit more for you. They're really open to your maybe going over for weekends, now and again, but if that's going to work, you really need to think about your behaviour.'

'I know.'

'The whole thing will break down if you decide to pour cement down their toilet or set fire to the curtains. Do you think you can keep yourself together?'

'I don't know. I'll have to try.'

I patted him on the shoulder. 'That's as much as anyone can do, I suppose.'

Edgar sighed. It was a tired, sad sound in the big empty church. 'Collette hasn't come back yet.'

'No.'

'Terri will be staying with that couple, won't she?'

'Yes, I think she will.'

He was quiet for a moment, then he said, 'I'm glad. She can grow up to be a nice kid. Not like me. Maybe if someone had loved me, I'd have been nice.'

'You still can be. You could start to treat people decently. That's pretty much what being nice is about.'

'I've been thinking about that. Oliver and I have been talking about it.'

'What does he think?'

'He says that people might give me a chance if I gave them a chance.'

'He's wise for such a little guy,' I said.

Edgar looked at me sharply, and I wondered if I had offended him. Then, without warning, he began to laugh. Luckily, we were the only ones in the church that afternoon, because Edgar's mirth was unrestrained. His face creased, tears rolled down his face and deep, hearty guffaws erupted from his throat. I watched him, bemused (the joke wasn't *that* funny) and delighted. I had feared, since the moment I had first met Edgar, that when he finally showed some emotion, it would be raw, uncontrollable rage. That his first expression of feelings was humour was a very pleasant surprise.

'He's smart all right,' Edgar managed to say at last. 'But then, he's always been able to *keep his head*.' And he was off again.

'Well, that's easy when you've got nobody to worry about,' I said.

You'd be amazed how many jokes we got out of Oliver Plunkett's unfortunate situation. As we sat there in the echoing marbled building, I could have sworn I saw a smile on the saint's face.

EPILOGUE

I parked the Austin by the kerb and looked at the name over the door of the small pub. This was the place.

The village was as I had expected it to be: a post office nestled on a bend in the road, and a grocery with a couple of petrol pumps was opposite. There were two or three houses dotted here and there, and a heavy smell of honeysuckle was in the air. A small church sat on a low hill, overlooking the cluster of dwellings; the headstones from its graveyard were silhouetted against the blue, cloudless sky. It had taken me three hours to drive there, and I had gotten lost twice.

It was one-thirty in the afternoon when I walked into the bar and pulled up a high stool. There were three old men sitting by the window, playing cards, and an elderly woman dozing in an armchair by the fire, a milk stout half drunk in front of her. Behind the bar was a man who could have been anything from fifty to seventy. He was probably six feet five inches, and had broad shoulders and a full head of white hair. He was very neatly dressed, with a crisp white shirt, a red tie and black and blue braces. A thick, well-groomed moustache nestled under his nose, which was long and looked as if it had been broken several times over the course of its life.

'What can I get you, sir?' he asked me, smiling.

'Do you have any non-alcoholic beers?' I asked, making a steering motion in the air.

'We have Becks, if that'll do you.'

'Becks is fine.'

'Will you take a glass and some ice?'

'Please.'

He put the drink in front of me. I paid him and took my change, and then he continued to wipe down the dark, wooden bar.

'So, what brings you to this part of the world?' he asked pleasantly. 'We get mostly locals in here, and you're not one, if you don't mind me saying so.'

'Not at all.' I grinned. This was pleasant—two guys, shooting the breeze on a sunny afternoon. 'A friend told me about this pub, actually, and I always said that if I was in the neighbourhood, I'd check it out.'

'Really? Now what friend would that be?'

'Oh, I doubt that you'd remember her. She moved away a long time ago.'

Behind me, the door creaked open, and I heard a high-pitched giggle. Looking over my shoulder, I caught sight of a rosy-cheeked face and a head of blonde ringlets peeping into the room. A smile spread across the man's face.

'Now what are you up to, Imelda?' he asked. 'Where's your mother?'

The door opened a bit wider, and a woman appeared. 'Sorry, Jamesie. I was just on my way to the shop, and she got away from me. Had to come in and see her pal, she did.'

'Sure, why don't you send her in for a glass of orange later, and you can pop over to Maggie's for a cup of tea? She can keep me company. It'll be quiet in here until they start coming home from work.'

'Are you sure?' the woman asked.

'I'm certain. You'll come in for a visit with your uncle James, won't you, Imelda?'

The child, who was probably three, giggled again. 'Yeah,' she said, and scuttled behind her mother's legs.

'Okay. I'll drop her off in half an hour or so,' the woman said, and went out.

'A relative of yours?' I asked, sipping my drink. Non-alcoholic beer isn't really beer at all. It's just a fizzy drink that makes you feel like a grown-up. I wasn't in the mood for something like orange or Coke. Not in that pub.

'No,' Jamesie said. 'A lot of the kids from the village come in and out of here. When you're in the country like we are, the pub has to serve the entire community. I encourage the little ones to come and go as they please. I like having them about.'

'Yes, Melanie told me as much,' I said.

I thought I caught a flicker in his eye when I said the name, but I couldn't be sure.

'Melanie?' he said. 'Now, do I remember a Melanie?'

'She certainly remembers you,' I said. 'Melanie Moorehouse. She has a little sister, Yasmin. She used to come and see you, too.'

He shook his head and began to unload the dishwasher. 'Sorry. I've been running this pub for forty years. So many people have been through, young and old, I couldn't possibly recollect them all.'

I tapped out a cigarette from my packet and lit it with my Zippo. 'You know, I made a few telephone calls before I drove out here today,' I said. 'And I sent some emails too.'

'Did you now? I'm not au fait with those computers,' he said. He had his back to me as he placed the clean glasses on their respective shelves.

'Oh, it's just like sending a letter, really, except they get to their destination much faster. See, I sent a report, written by Melanie Moorehouse, to the social work team leader for this region. It contained details of how you abused her and her sister over a period of two years. She also listed the names of other children she knows were regular visitors to the pub during her time here. I reckon they'd be easy enough to trace—small communities like this, everyone knows where people go. I rang the social work office this morning to make sure they'd got that report okay, and sure enough, they had. They're very interested in its contents, and will be investigating it enthusiastically. Melanie's a social worker herself now, you see, and those guys tend to look after one of their own.'

He had stopped stacking glasses. He was leaning against the worktop on his side of the bar, and I could see his shoulders moving up and down as he breathed.

'Of course, child sexual abuse is a criminal offence,' I continued, 'and I couldn't just tell social services. So I rang the Gardai in the next town over, too. I let them know that I'd be visiting you, but they'll want to talk to you themselves. Probably this evening. The cops tend to take paedophilia quite seriously.'

'You should leave now,' he said, 'before I throw you out.'

He was maybe forty years older than me, but I guessed he could make a fair go of it.

'I'm going,' I said. 'I just wanted to deliver the message in person. It's a problem a lot of kids have, when some scumbag molests them. They feel isolated, as if nobody gives a damn about them. People like you, Jamesie, you capitalise on that. Well, I'm here to let you know—I fucking care. I give a damn. You hurt my friend, and I suspect you've been hurting children in this place for decades.'

'Get out,' he said again.

'It stops now, Jamesie,' I said. 'I'll be keeping a very close eye on what goes on in this village. I'll make sure the case is pushed as far as it can go. You're going to do jail time, Jamesie. I promise you that.'

I stood up and stubbed out my cigarette in an ashtray. 'I think you should close up for the afternoon,' I said. 'I don't reckon it would be a good idea for Imelda to come here, do you?'

I left him standing there in his dark, shiny bar, and pulled the front door shut behind me.

When I was back in the Austin, I rolled down the windows and found a Chuck Berry tape for the drive home. The road ahead was difficult in places, but it was a beautiful day.

AFTERWORD

The book you've just read contains stories taken from right across my career in social care. While I have had to alter details to protect the anonymity of those involved, everything I describe really happened.

In *Boy in the Cupboard*, I ostensibly set out to tell the stories of Litovoi Tomescu and Edgar O'Sullivan, but as the book progressed, those cases began to stretch and become more complex. I found Litovoi's tale jostling for space with that of Gregor and Vladimir Blerinca, and Edgar's story came to involve Melanie Moorehouse, and, of course, Collette and little Terri.

And others found their way in, also: Hugh Whitty and David; Cezar; Karl Devereux; Patience; St Oliver Plunkett; even Anansi and Turtle—all these people stole into the book, and enriched it in their own way. But I do not see them as thieves in the night— they belong here. Child-protection cases are almost always complex, multi-layered things, and *Boy in the Cupboard* is a testament to that.

The Tomescu family were happy and living comfortably, the last time I heard from them. I do not know what role Petru is playing in Gregor Blerinca's affairs, and have no desire to find out.

Vladimir Blerinca—Vinnie—went on to study journalism. He worked for a time for a gay publication in Dublin, and then moved to the United States where he continues to work in publishing. Homosexuality proved to be a part of who he is, rather than a phase, and it seems that Gregor accepted that, even if he was never very happy about it.

Edgar O'Sullivan remains one of the children I worked with with whom I never managed to establish a relationship. I finished seeing him shortly after the events recounted in this book, and our parting was, to say the least, apathetic.

Edgar, always a peculiar child, managed to compartmentalise his behaviour. He was very pleasant to Terri's foster family, while he continued his reign of terror at Bluecloud. That placement eventually broke down, and Edgar was transferred to a high support unit (a lock-up, for want of a better word), which represented a complete failure on my part.

From what I can gather, a worker at the high support managed to achieve what had confounded all the other professionals who had tried to help Edgar before, and formed a friendship with him. This relationship proved to be hugely beneficial, and the boy returned to Bluecloud after a year completely changed. A close friend of mine works with him now (he is twenty-one years old as I write this, and in college), and she tells me regularly how much she loves him. I am glad. Love might have saved him, had he received the right kind early in his life. It is an unequivocal belief of mine that love is a basic human right—children, in particular, are entitled to it. It is a great tragedy that Edgar O'Sullivan had to be in his teens before he found someone who could genuinely appreciate him, but better late than never.

Edgar and Terri remain close.

Collette returned to the city almost a year later, and was prosecuted for abandonment. She testified that Marius had coerced her into leaving the baby, and she received a suspended sentence. She made no effort to get custody of Terri again. She has access visits with both children weekly.

Melanie Moorehouse is still a social worker, and a very fine one. We are no longer as close as we once were—life has conspired against us, and our paths rarely cross now, but when they do, we are lucky enough to be able to pick up where we left off—our friendship has the elasticity.

Melanie stopped working in social care for two years, while she attended counselling, for both alcohol addiction and the sexual abuse. 'I wouldn't say I'm recovered,' she told me the other day. 'I'm in recovery. And that's enough, for now.'

Her abuser, Jamesie, never did do any jail time. A judge decided that at seventy-five he was too old to be a threat, and, like Collette, he received a suspended sentence and was placed on probation. Three months later, he died of a heart attack. They tell me his funeral was the biggest the village had ever seen.

Published in September 2010

WILL MAMMY BE COMING BACK FOR ME?
by
Shane Dunphy

I sat opposite Garda Miriam Kelleher in the squad room of the crowded local police station. There was very little floor space, as the room had been packed to capacity with desks and chairs, and the narrow passageways that did exist between the workstations were clogged with boxes of files and other assorted detritus. The sound of the radio crackling into life every few moments punctuated the buzz of conversation.

'He's asking for you,' Miriam said. She was taller than me, with square glasses and dark blonde hair tied in a loose ponytail. She had worked for a time as a residential childcare worker, and therefore caught a lot of the juvenile liaison cases.

'I *will* go and talk with him, Midge, but I need to know what I'm dealing with,' I said. I had drunk too much coffee—even for me—and felt tired and jittery. I wished I was at home, but I knew I wouldn't rest until I had found some answers. The only person who could provide them was locked in a nearby cell. 'I remember this kid as a terrified five-year-old. I'm guessing there's been a lot of water under the bridge since then.'

Miriam pushed a heavy file across her desk towards me. 'Gallons,' she said.

I looked at the ream of paper and sighed, deeply.

'Can't you summarise it for me?'

'Okay, then. In brief, Jason Farrell is about as bad a kid as you could hope to come across,' Miriam said, observing me wince but continuing mercilessly. 'He has been involved in a variety of petty crimes, most of them involving violence of one kind or another. It's only a matter of time before he graduates on to something more serious, and someone dies. He's been caught with firearms twice, and we suspect he's on the perimeter of at least one of the local gangs. He's certainly been seen in the company of some of their lower ranking members.' She sat back and let that information sink in. 'For that alone, I'd be glad to see him put away for a long while.'

'But there's more?' I prompted.

She flipped open the file, and riffled through it to a heavily lined page.

'In 1997, when he was eleven, Jason Farrell took a three-year-old girl, Mary Connors, into a field behind the halting site, an official area for Travellers where her family were staying, and molested her. I won't disturb you with the gory details—suffice it to say it was sadistic enough to have him placed in a secure care institution for a year after that. They released him, and put him under the watchful eye of a foster family, but obviously before he was ready. In 1999, he broke into the house of a neighbour, and violently sexually abused their two-year-old daughter.'

'If he's such a serious threat, how come he's still at large?' I asked impatiently. 'Why the fuck is he arriving at my office and beating up my friends?'

'Shane, you'd be the first person to advocate kids getting a second chance, even the really messed up ones,' Miriam shot back. 'He was put in a programme for young offenders. It seemed to be working, the second time around. He was sent back home to his birth parents in the Oldtown.'

I sighed. 'I can guess that didn't go well.'

'A couple of complaints came in about him hanging around the local primary school,' Miriam said. 'I had a talk with him, that time, warned him off. Then we got a call about a little girl who had been approached by a man when she was out playing. This guy wanted her to go for a walk with him. He said he'd buy her a new doll. Thankfully, she was well aware of "stranger danger", and ran and told her parents. Our boy swears blind it wasn't him, and I won't make a four-year-old pick him out of a line-up, so we let that one lie. But last week, there was a burglary—an old woman who lived in the flats. She was in bed, and when she got up to confront the intruders, one of them dragged her back into her room and sexually assaulted her. This is an eighty-year-old woman, mind. Even though he was wearing a balaclava, she was able to give us enough information to identify Jason.'

'How?'

'Indian-ink tattoos on his hand. Unmistakable. He's going down, this time.'

'He's still only sixteen. That's a child, the last time I looked.'

'He's been kept out of the really serious juvenile detention centres before now. But not any more. He's a serial offender, Shane, and a fucking menace to society. Do you want to see a photo of that old lady's face? He bruised it up pretty good. Bit her cheek so badly she needed stitches. I could give you a description of the genital scarring.'

I shook my head. 'No thanks.'

'He might have only been a pup when you last saw him,' Miriam said, 'but he's grown into a fucking Rottweiler. There's nothing any of us can do, now, except put him where he isn't a danger to anyone.'

I rubbed my eyes. 'Can I go and talk to him?'

Miriam sat back and put her hands behind her head. I could see her biceps flex beneath her blue shirt. She was a pretty girl, but it would have been a mistake to think that was all she was. 'Are you sure you want to?'

'I guess I owe it to him.'

'Why? What good will it do?'

'Dunno. But it can't hurt, can it?'

She shrugged. 'Your funeral. Come on then.'